PSALTER

FOR THE
CHRISTIAN PEOPLE

An Inclusive-Language Revision
of the Psalter
of The Book of Common Prayer 1979

edited by
Gordon Lathrop
and
Gail Ramshaw

A PUEBLO BOOK

The Liturgical Press   Collegeville, Minnesota

A Pueblo Book published by The Liturgical Press

Design by Frank Kacmarcik, Obl.S.B.

1   2   3   4   5   6   7   8   9

Library of Congress Cataloging-in-Publication Data

Episcopal Church. Book of common prayer (1979). Psalter.
   Psalter for the Christian people : an inclusive-language revision
of the Psalter of the Book of common prayer 1979 / edited by Gordon
Lathrop and Gail Ramshaw.
       p.   cm.
   "A Pueblo book."
   ISBN 0-8146-6134-3
   I. Lathrop, Gordon. II. Ramshaw, Gail, 1947- . III. Title.
BX5146.A1 1993
264'.038—dc20   93-10817
                                                           CIP

Contents

Introduction

In 1986–88, aware that the Sunday readings needed to be available in inclusive language, Pueblo Publishing Company published the *Lectionary for the Christian People*, the Roman, Episcopal, and Lutheran lectionaries in an emended form of the Revised Standard Version. More recently, the increasing desire among Christians in North America to pray in inclusive language has resulted in several new translations of the Psalter, each attempting this difficult task with different techniques. With this volume, the editors of the *Lectionary for the Christian People* present an inclusive language Psalter. Many Christians, including several entire church bodies, have come to revere the Psalter translation in the 1979 *Book of Common Prayer*; for example, it is the Psalter translation included in the 1978 *Lutheran Book of Worship*. For this reason we have based this rendering on the BCP Psalter, with hopes that its familiar cadence adapted in a nuanced manner will fill the needs of many. In keeping with the intent of the BCP Psalter, every effort has been made to render the lines in a euphonious manner, well phrased for chanting. Because different communions practice variant methods of chanting, this volume includes an essay which offers instruction in four methods of pointing these psalms.

The principles of this revision are as follows:

1. The use of "LORD" as the translation of the tetragrammaton and "Lord" as the translation of *Adonai* have been retained.

2. The metaphor "king" when referring to God has been rendered "Sovereign" and God's "kingdom" as God's "reign."

3. Masculine pronouns referring to God have been eliminated.

4. In any psalm which in the Hebrew uses both "God" and "LORD" as divine designations, this revision alternates these titles as one technique to eliminate the masculine pronoun.

5. Hebrew poetry allows a switching of grammatical person (i.e., from "you," second person, to "he, she, it, they," third person) in a manner considered grammatically unacceptable in modern English. Some biblical scholars suggest that this alternation of person provides a meaningful distinction between proclamation (God as third person) and prayer (God as second person). The editors of this volume find this distinction strained and unsupportable by the Hebrew itself. Rather, person in ancient Hebrew was grammatically fluid. This fact allows modern liturgical usage to substitute second person (God as you) in some cases as a technique to eliminate masculine pronouns. The rule of this revision is to make such substitutions only in those psalms that already include second person in the original Hebrew.

6. The masculine possessive pronoun when referring to God has been rendered in several ways. Substitutions for "his" include "the holy," as in "the holy angels"; "the chosen," as in "the chosen people"; "divine," as in "divine rage"; "of the LORD," as in "the commandments of the LORD"; "God's," as in "God's holy heaven." Occasionally the context allows the possessive form to be dropped.

7. The masculine objective pronoun when referring to God has been rendered in several ways. "Praise him" becomes "give praise"; "bow before him" becomes "bow in worship"; "call upon him" becomes "cry out"; "those who fear him" becomes "the God-fearing"; "revealed himself" becomes "appeared."

8. While the original BCP translation already dealt with many masculine passages meant to be generic (for example, the BCP casts Psalm 1 in the plural), some more adaptations in human language have been made.

9. In several cases the gender of the metaphor is an essential aspect of the poem. For example, Psalm 45 is an epithalamion for a king and a princess. No attempt has been made to make such inclusive. The churches must decide in what contexts these psalms are appropriate prayer.

10. The following are commonly recurring alterations: brother, brethren = kin, family, community; the city = rendered as "it"; daughter of X = city of X (as already in Psalm 9:14); forefather = ancestor; Jacob and Israel = rendered in the plural; king = ruler,

king; kingdom = realm; maiden = young woman; prince = noble; watchman = sentry.

All these techniques are applications of a liturgical principle taught us by the ancient Hebrew people themselves. Although their written texts spelled out the name of God, we know that in the liturgical assembly the people substituted a circumlocution for that mysterious name, as if human pronunciation of God's name would tarnish its majesty. For those Christians who now believe that suggesting divine masculinity similarly mars our worship, we offer this revision of the BCP Psalter.

Gordon Lathrop
Gail Ramshaw

Singing the Psalter

Much has been said and written about the unique gift of sung psalmody to the Church, especially in the last twenty years. With the publication of many hymnals and books of worship across many communions, the Christian assemblies have encountered systems of tones that allow for the regular practice of chanting the psalms. Now, in this time of growing familiarity with each book's system of chant, many congregations and parishes cry out for a more varied approach. It is for this reason that the *Psalter for the Christian People* comes in a form without pointing that conforms to a certain system. With some time and care, this revision of the Psalter can be pointed in the manner of any of these conventional methods, allowing for flexibility and diversity.

The most common musical systems for chanting psalmody today are the single and double tones available in the *Lutheran Book of Worship* and *Lutheran Worship,* the Anglican chant practice as found in *The Anglican Chant Psalter,* and the plainsong psalm tones as collected in *The Plainsong Psalter.* All of these systems employ "pointing," a method of indicating pitch modifications through a series of points, dashes, and dots, to make a series of musical tones interchangeable with the full Psalter. The Lutheran and Anglican versions tend to be more interchangeable than the plainsong formulas, due to the endless variables and options available to the plainsong tone singers. And yet, this palette of possibilities is just the remedy needed to cure the passive droning of the many assemblies who have fallen into the habit of using just two or three, or worse, only one tone from week to week.

In order to make use of these varied formulas, one must become familiar with the patterns and guidelines for pointing in each system. Pointing relies on understanding word and syllable stress and placing accents, dots, and dashes in the appropriate places to match the tones in question. By following the guidelines for pointing in the manner of the three systems below, the possibilities for varied chanting are nearly endless. We begin first with the simplest of pointing systems, that of the chanting formulas used in the *Lutheran Book of Worship* and *Lutheran Worship*.

LBW psalm tones are either single (two measures) or double (four measures) tones. *LW* tones are all single, two-measure tones. In any of these cases, each verse of the psalm is sung to two matched groupings made up of a reciting tone and a three-note cadence. The midpoint of each verse corresponding with the parallel nature of most psalm verses is indicated by the asterisk. An accent over the syllable in which the three note cadence begins is placed on the *second syllable prior to the last accented syllable of each half-verse*. For example, the accent placements for Psalm 18:34-38 are as follows:

34 You make me sure-footed like a deer *

     and let me stand firm ón the heights.

35 You train my hands for battle *

     and my arms for bending even a bow of bronze.

36 You have given me your shield of victory; *

     your right hand also sustains me;

     your loving care mákes me great.

37 You lengthen my stride beneath me, *

     and my ankles do nót give way.

38 I pursue my enemies and óvertake them; *

     I will not turn back till I háve destroyed them.

Notice that in verse 35 ''battle'' is a two-syllable word with the accent on the first syllable. Therefore the point is placed on the second syllable prior to the syllable ''bat-.'' The more difficult pointing can be noticed in verses 37 and 38. In the first half-verse of both of these verses, the final one syllable word is an unstressed word in normal speech patterns. In these cases, the point is placed before the second syllable prior to the accented syllable

2

of the stronger words "beneath" and "overtake." In a very few cases, some verses end with two unaccented words, and in these cases the same rules apply.

LBW double tones work with this same pointing practice. In the case of a double tone, however, two verses are used with the four-measure units. It is advisable to use psalms with an even number of verses so that these double tones will end on the root chords.

LW tones are all single tones but differ musically from the *LBW* tones. The difference in the pointing system of *LW* is that the *point is always placed on the second last or third last syllables*. A vertical point over the third last syllable indicates that the three notes of the musical cadence are sung to the last three syllables of the verse, while a horizontal point over the second last syllable indicates that the three notes of the musical cadence are sung to the last two syllables, with the first of these syllables sung on a slur of two notes. Again as an example note the difference in pointing with Psalm 18:34-38:

34 You make me sure-footed like a deer *

    and let me stand firm on the heights.

35 You train my hands for battle *

    and my arms for bending even a bow of bronze.

36 You have given me your shield of victory; *

    your right hand also sustains me;

    your loving care makes me great.

37 You lengthen my stride beneath me, *

    and my ankles do not give way.

38 I pursue my enemies and overtake them; *

    I will not turn back till I have destroyed them.

The musical tones for psalms are printed on page 291 of the pew edition of the *Lutheran Book of Worship* and pages 367–68 of *Lutheran Worship*. While both collections are under copyright, permission can easily be obtained to reprint these tones in worship bulletins by calling the publishers of each worship book. Another possibility is for musicians to compose their own single and double tones to use with this pointing system.

The use of harmonized psalm tones known as Anglican chant is another popular way to chant psalmody. While more complex than the Lutheran double and single tones, Anglican chant has been used with great success across denominational lines. Again, the process of pointing relies on placing the dashes, dots, and brackets in the verses to make it possible to sing the texts to the many available tones.

Anglican pointing uses a vertical point before the stressed syllables to be sung to the various chords of the chant. The beginning of each half verse is sung monotone on the opening chord until the first vertical point occurs. Then syllables are sung to the successive chords that follow. In some cases, two or three syllables meant to be sung on one chord are indicated by a horizontal bracket above the syllables. Also, one syllable may be marked to be sung to two chords with two dots over the syllable. An asterisk dividing the verse in half is used in Anglican Chant as it is in the Lutheran tones. A more complete discussion of the Anglican pointing system is available in the preface to *The Anglican Chant Psalter* published by The Church Hymnal Corporation and edited by Alec Wyton.

The placement of the vertical points for the first half-verse is similar to Lutheran pointing. By placing a vertical line prior to both the second last and the last stressed syllable of the half-verse, the opening reciting chord and the three chords that follow have been used. The second half-verse is twice as long, so it requires a third vertical line. In this case, a vertical line is placed prior to the third last, second last, and last stressed syllables of the half-verse. Place the horizontal bracket or dots over syllables to make them correspond to the chords of the chant. As an example, note again Psalm 18:34-38 pointed for Anglican chant:

34 You make me sure-footed like a deer *

    and let me stand firm on the heights.

35 You train my hands for battle *

    and my arms for bending even a bow of bronze.

4

36 You have given me your‖shield‖of victory; *

   your right hand also sustains me;

   your loving‖care‖makes me great.

37 You lengthen my‖stride beneath me, *

   and my‖ankles do‖not give‖way.

38 I pursue my enemies and‖overtake them; *

   I will not turn‖back till I‖have destroyed them.

The Anglican Chant Psalter contains an exhaustive collection of psalm tones, many of which are in public domain. Permission can be obtained to reprint those still remaining under copyright by calling the publisher.

Pointing for plainsong chant is the most complex of the available pointing systems due to the wide number of possible variations on the basic tones. The basic tones with their possible endings are printed on pages 319–24 in *The Plainsong Psalter* and may be reprinted with permission. The full process of pointing psalms in this manner is much too complex for this preface, but with careful examination of the possible tones and a process of "trial and error," these time-weathered tones could be very usable in the liturgy today.

Beyond the diversity of tones and pointing systems, psalm singing can be enlivened by varying the voices. Boredom is near for those who use responsive chant (cantor vs. congregation) exclusively. The use of antiphonal chant (left side vs. right side, choir vs. congregation, men vs. women and children, etc.) might be the only variation needed to regenerate interest in psalm singing. Adding an antiphon (refrain) at the beginning, ending, and throughout the psalm can also break monotony and focus the textual emphasis of the psalm.

In addition to varying the psalm format for singing, attention always needs to be paid to the style of the singing itself. Good chanting is good singing, but it is more like good speaking. Assemblies should be given the freedom to breathe and pause as they would when speaking in unison and allowed to shape the words in rhythmic patterns that we all customarily use in public speech. It is only when chant resembles speech that the music will get out of the way for the words to live in the deepest reaches of the heart.

To show these various possibilities in full use, Psalm 82 is presented below in four varying styles. The first is the type found in the Lutheran worship books with an antiphon, the second in Anglican chant, the third in a plainsong formula with an antiphon, and the last in a hybrid of all types. It is through the creative use of these various formats that a new excitement for sung psalmody will be sparked in our Christian gatherings.

Mark Mummert
The Holy Innocents, December 28, 1992

+ Psalm 82 +

Antiphon

A - rise, O God, and rule the earth.

Psalm Tone

Antiphon

1 God arises in the council of heaven *

   and gives judgment in the midst óf the gods:

2 "How long will you júdge unjustly, *

   and show favor tó the wicked?

3 Save the weak añd the orphan; *

   defend the humble and needy;

4 Rescue the weak ánd the poor; *

   deliver them from the power óf the wicked. (Antiphon)

5 They do not know, neither do they understand;

   they go abóut in darkness; *

   all the foundations of the eárth are shaken.

6 Now I say to you, 'You are gods, *

   and all of you children of the Most High;

7 Nevertheless, you shall die like mortals, *

   and fall like ány leader.' "

8 Arise, O God and rúle the earth, *

   for you shall take all nations fór your own. (Antiphon)

+ Psalm 82 +

R.P. Stewart

Psalm Tone

1 God arises in the 'council of 'heaven *
   and gives 'judgment in the 'midst of the 'gods:

2 "How long will you 'judge unjustly, *
   and show 'favor 'to the 'wicked?

3 Save the 'weak and the 'orphan; *
   defend the 'humble and 'needy;

4 Rescue the 'weak and the 'poor; *
   deliver them from the 'power 'of the 'wicked. (Antiphon)

5 They do not know, neither do they understand;
   they go about in 'darkness; *
   all the foundations of the 'earth are 'shaken.

6 Now I say to you, ' 'You are 'gods, *
   and all of you 'children of the 'Most 'High;

7 Nevertheless, you shall 'die like 'mortals, *
   and 'fall like 'any 'leader.' "

8 Arise, O God and 'rule the 'earth, *
   for you shall take all 'nations 'for your 'own. (Antiphon)

+ Psalm 82 +

Antiphon

A - rise,　　O God,　and rule　　the earth.

Psalm Tone

1　God arises in the council of héaven *
　　and gives judgment in the mídst of the gods:
2　"How long will you judge unjústly, *
　　and show favór to the wicked?
3　Save the weak and the órphan; *
　　defend the humble and néedy;
4　Rescue the weak and the póor; *
　　deliver them from the power óf the wicked. (Antiphon)
5　They do not know, neither do they understand;
　　they go about in dárkness; *
　　all the foundations of the eárth are shaken.
6　Now I say to you, 'You are góds, *
　　and all of you children óf the Most High;
7　Nevertheless, you shall die like mórtals, *
　　and fall like ány léader.' "
8　Arise, O God and rule the éarth, *
　　for you shall take all natións for your own. (Antiphon)

+ Psalm 82 +

A - rise, O God, and rule the earth.

Psalm Tone

1 God arises in the council of heaven *
     and gives judgment in the midst óf the gods:
2 "How long will you júdge unjustly, *
     and show favor tó the wicked?
3 Save the weak añd the orphan; *
     defend the humble and needy;
4 Rescue the weak ánd the poor; *
     deliver them from the power óf the wicked. (Antiphon)

5 They do not know, neither do they understand;
   they go abóut in darkness; *

   all the foundations of the eárth are shaken.

6 Now I say to you, 'Yóu are gods, *

   and all of you children of the Most High;

7 Nevertheless, you shall díe like mortals, *

   and fall like ány leader.' "

8 Arise, O God and rúle the earth, *

   for you shall take all nations fór your own. (Antiphon)

1

1 Happy are they who have not walked in the counsel of the
    wicked, *
    nor lingered in the way of sinners,
    nor sat in the seats of the scornful!

2 Their delight is in the law of the LORD, *
    and on this law they meditate day and night.

3 They are like trees planted by streams of water,
    bearing fruit in due season, with leaves that do not wither; *
    everything they do shall prosper.

4 It is not so with the wicked; *
    they are like chaff which the wind blows away.

5 Therefore the wicked shall not stand upright when judgment
    comes, *
    nor the sinner in the council of the righteous.

6 For the LORD knows the way of the righteous, *
    but the way of the wicked is doomed.

2

1 Why are the nations in an uproar? *
    Why do the peoples mutter empty threats?

2 Why do the kings of the earth rise up in revolt,
    and the rulers plot together, *
    against the LORD and against the LORD's anointed?

3 "Let us break their yoke," they say; *
    "let us cast off their bonds from us."

4 The One enthroned in heaven is laughing; *
    the Lord has them in derision.

5 Then in wrath the LORD speaks to them, *
    and divine rage fills them with terror.

6 "I myself have set my king *
    upon my holy hill of Zion."

7   Let me announce the decree of the LORD: *
      the LORD said to me, "You are my son;
      this day have I begotten you.

8   Ask of me, and I will give you the nations for your inheritance *
      and the ends of the earth for your possession.

9   You shall crush them with an iron rod *
      and shatter them like a piece of pottery."

10   And now, you kings, be wise; *
      be warned, you rulers of the earth.

11   Submit to the LORD with fear, *
      and with trembling bow down in worship;

12   Lest the LORD be angry and you perish; *
      for divine wrath is quickly kindled.

13   Happy are they all *
      who take refuge in the LORD!

3

1   LORD, how many adversaries I have! *
      how many there are who rise up against me!

2   How many there are who say to me, *
      "There is no help for you in your God."

3   But you, O LORD, are a shield about me; *
      you are my glory, the one who lifts up my head.

4   I call aloud to you, O LORD, *
      and you answer me from your holy hill;

5   I lie down and go to sleep; *
      I wake again, because the LORD sustains me.

6   I do not fear the multitudes of people *
      who set themselves against me all around.

7   Rise up, O LORD; set me free, O my God; *
      surely, you will strike all my enemies across the face,
      you will break the teeth of the wicked.

8 Deliverance belongs to the LORD. *
    Your blessing be upon your people!

4

1 Answer me when I call, O God, defender of my cause; *
    you set me free when I am hard-pressed;
    have mercy on me and hear my prayer.

2 "You mortals, how long will you dishonor my glory; *
    how long will you worship dumb idols
    and run after false gods?"

3 Know that the LORD does wonders for the faithful; *
    when I cry out, the LORD will hear me.

4 Tremble, then, and do not sin; *
    speak to your heart in silence upon your bed.

5 Offer the appointed sacrifices *
    and put your trust in the LORD.

6 Many are saying, "Oh, that we might see better times!" *
    Lift up the light of your countenance upon us, O LORD.

7 You have put gladness in my heart, *
    more than when grain and wine and oil increase.

8 I lie down in peace; at once I fall asleep; *
    for only you, LORD, make me dwell in safety.

5

1 Give ear to my words, O LORD; *
    consider my meditation.

2 Hearken to my cry for help, my Sovereign and my God, *
    for I make my prayer to you.

3 In the morning, LORD, you hear my voice; *
    early in the morning I make my appeal and watch for you.

4 For you are not a God who takes pleasure in wickedness, *
    and evil cannot dwell with you.

5 Braggarts cannot stand in your sight; *
   you hate all those who work wickedness.

6 You destroy those who speak lies; *
   the bloodthirsty and deceitful, O LORD, you abhor.

7 But as for me, through the greatness of your mercy I will go
      into your house; *
   I will bow down toward your holy temple in awe of you.

8 Lead me, O LORD, in your righteousness,
   because of those who lie in wait for me; *
   make your way straight before me.

9 For there is no truth in their mouth; *
   there is destruction in their heart;

10 Their throat is an open grave; *
   they flatter with their tongue.

11 Declare them guilty, O God; *
   let them fall, because of their schemes.

12 Because of their many transgressions cast them out, *
   for they have rebelled against you.

13 But all who take refuge in you will be glad; *
   they will sing out their joy for ever.

14 You will shelter them, *
   so that those who love your name may exult in you.

15 For you, O LORD, will bless the righteous; *
   you will defend them with your favor as with a shield.

6

1 LORD, do not rebuke me in your anger; *
   do not punish me in your wrath.

2 Have pity on me, LORD, for I am weak; *
   heal me, LORD, for my bones are racked.

3 My spirit shakes with terror; *
   how long, O LORD, how long?

4 Turn, O Lord, and deliver me; *
　　save me for your mercy's sake.

5 For in death no one remembers you; *
　　and who will give you thanks in the grave?

6 I grow weary because of my groaning; *
　　every night I drench my bed
　　and flood my couch with tears.

7 My eyes are wasted with grief *
　　and worn away because of all my enemies.

8 Depart from me, all evildoers, *
　　for the Lord has heard the sound of my weeping.

9 The Lord has heard my supplication; *
　　the Lord accepts my prayer.

10 All my enemies shall be confounded and quake with fear; *
　　they shall turn back and suddenly be put to shame.

7

1 O Lord my God, I take refuge in you; *
　　save and deliver me from all who pursue me;

2 Lest like a lion they tear me in pieces *
　　and snatch me away with none to deliver me.

3 O Lord my God, if I have done these things: *
　　if there is any wickedness in my hands,

4 If I have repaid my friend with evil, *
　　or plundered anyone who without cause is my enemy;

5 Then let my enemy pursue and overtake me, *
　　trample my life into the ground,
　　and lay my honor in the dust.

6 Stand up, O Lord, in your wrath; *
　　rise up against the fury of my enemies.

7 Awake, O my God, decree justice; *
　　let the assembly of the peoples gather round you.

8 Be seated on your lofty throne, O Most High; *
   O LORD, judge the nations.

9 Give judgment for me according to my righteousness, O LORD, *
   and according to my innocence, O Most High.

10 Let the malice of the wicked come to an end,
   but establish the righteous; *
      for you test the mind and heart, O righteous God.

11 God is my shield and defense, *
   the savior of the true in heart.

12 God is a righteous judge; *
   God sits in judgment every day.

13 If they will not repent, God will whet a sword, *
   bending a bow and making it ready.

14 God has prepared weapons of death, *
   making arrows into shafts of fire.

15 Look at those who are in labor with wickedness, *
   who conceive evil, and give birth to a lie.

16 They dig a pit and make it deep *
   and fall into the hole that they have made.

17 Their malice turns back upon their own head; *
   their violence falls on their own scalp.

18 I will bear witness that the LORD is righteous; *
   I will praise the name of the LORD Most High.

8

1 O LORD our Lord, *
   how exalted is your name in all the world!

2 Out of the mouths of infants and children *
   your majesty is praised above the heavens.

3 You have set up a stronghold against your adversaries, *
   to quell the enemy and the avenger.

4 When I consider your heavens, the work of your fingers, *
    the moon and the stars you have set in their courses,

5 What are human beings that you should be mindful of them? *
    mortals that you should seek them out?

6 You have made them but little lower than the angels; *
    you adorn them with glory and honor;

7 You give them mastery over the works of your hands; *
    you put all things under their feet:

8 All sheep and oxen, *
    even the wild beasts of the field,

9 The birds of the air, the fish of the sea, *
    and whatsoever walks in the paths of the sea.

10 O LORD our Lord, *
    how exalted is your name in all the world!

9

1 I will give thanks to you, O LORD, with my whole heart; *
    I will tell of all your marvelous works.

2 I will be glad and rejoice in you; *
    I will sing to your name, O Most High.

3 When my enemies are driven back, *
    they will stumble and perish at your presence.

4 For you have maintained my right and my cause; *
    you sit upon your throne judging right.

5 You have rebuked the ungodly and destroyed the wicked; *
    you have blotted out their name for ever and ever.

6 As for the enemy, they are finished, in perpetual ruin, *
    their cities ploughed under, the memory of them perished;

7 But you, O LORD, are enthroned for ever; *
    you have set up your throne for judgment.

8 It is you who rule the world with righteousness; *
    you judge the peoples with equity.

9 The LORD will be a refuge for the oppressed, *
     a refuge in time of trouble.

10 Those who know your name will put their trust in you, *
     for you never forsake those who seek you, O LORD.

11 Sing praise to the LORD who dwells in Zion; *
     proclaim to the peoples the things the LORD has done.

12 The Avenger of blood will remember them, *
     and will not forget the cry of the afflicted.

13 Have pity on me, O LORD; *
     see the misery I suffer from those who hate me,
     O you who lift me up from the gate of death;

14 So that I may tell of all your praises
     and rejoice in your salvation *
     in the gates of the city of Zion.

15 The ungodly have fallen into the pit they dug, *
     and in the snare they set is their own foot caught.

16 The LORD is known by divine acts of justice; *
     the wicked are trapped in the works of their own hands.

17 The wicked shall be given over to the grave, *
     and also all the peoples that forget God.

18 For the needy shall not always be forgotten, *
     and the hope of the poor shall not perish for ever.

19 Rise up, O LORD, let not the ungodly have the upper hand; *
     let them be judged before you.

20 Put fear upon them, O LORD; *
     let the ungodly know they are but mortal.

10

1 Why do you stand so far off, O LORD, *
     and hide yourself in time of trouble?

2 The wicked arrogantly persecute the poor, *
     but they are trapped in the schemes they have devised.

3 The wicked boast of their heart's desire; *
   the covetous curse and revile the LORD.

4 The wicked are so proud that they care not for God; *
   their only thought is, "God does not matter."

5 Their ways are devious at all times;
   your judgments are far above, out of their sight; *
   they defy all their enemies.

6 They say in their heart, "I shall not be shaken; *
   no harm shall happen to me ever."

7 Their mouth is full of cursing, deceit, and oppression; *
   under their tongue are mischief and wrong.

8 They lurk in ambush in public squares
   and in secret places they murder the innocent; *
   they spy out the helpless.

9 They lie in wait, like a lion in a covert;
   they lie in wait to seize upon the lowly; *
   they seize the lowly and drag them away in their net.

10 The innocent are broken and humbled before them; *
   the helpless fall before their power.

11 They say in their heart, "God has forgotten; *
   God's face is hidden; God will never notice."

12 Rise up, O LORD;
   lift up your hand, O God; *
   do not forget the afflicted.

13 Why should the wicked revile God? *
   why should they say in their heart that you do not care?

14 Surely, you behold trouble and misery; *
   you see it and take it into your own hand.

15 The helpless commit themselves to you, *
   for you are the helper of orphans.

16 Break the power of the wicked and evil; *
   search out their wickedness until you find none.

17 The LORD is Sovereign for ever and ever; *
   the ungodly shall perish from your land.

18 The LORD will hear the desire of the humble; *
   you will strengthen their heart and your ears shall hear;

19 To give justice to the orphan and oppressed, *
   so that mere mortals may strike terror no more.

11

1 In the LORD have I taken refuge; *
   how then can you say to me,
      "Fly away like a bird to the hilltop;

2 For see how the wicked bend the bow
   and fit their arrows to the string, *
      to shoot from ambush at the true of heart.

3 When the foundations are being destroyed, *
   what can the righteous do?"

4 The LORD is in the holy temple; *
   the LORD's throne is in heaven.

5 The LORD's eyes behold the inhabited world; *
   the LORD's piercing eye weighs our worth.

6 The LORD weighs the righteous as well as the wicked, *
   but abhors those who delight in violence.

7 Upon the wicked the LORD shall rain coals of fire and burning
      sulphur; *
   a scorching wind shall be their lot.

8 For the LORD, who is righteous,
   delights in righteous deeds; *
      and the just shall see the face of the LORD.

12

1 Help me, LORD, for there is no godly one left; *
   the faithful have vanished from among us.

2 All speak falsely with their neighbor; *
  with a smooth tongue they speak from a double heart.

3 Oh, that the LORD would cut off all smooth tongues, *
  and close the lips that utter proud boasts!

4 Those who say, "With our tongue will we prevail; *
  our lips are our own; who is lord over us?"

5 "Because the needy are oppressed,
  and the poor cry out in misery, *
    I will rise up," says the LORD,
    "and give them the help they long for."

6 The words of the LORD are pure words, *
  like silver refined from ore
  and purified seven times in the fire.

7 O LORD, watch over us *
  and save us from this generation for ever.

8 The wicked prowl on every side, *
  and that which is worthless is highly prized by everyone.

13

1 How long, O LORD?
  will you forget me for ever? *
    how long will you hide your face from me?

2 How long shall I have perplexity in my mind,
  and grief in my heart, day after day? *
    how long shall my enemy triumph over me?

3 Look upon me and answer me, O LORD my God; *
  give light to my eyes, lest I sleep in death;

4 Lest my enemy say, "I have prevailed," *
  and my foes rejoice that I have fallen.

5 But I put my trust in your mercy; *
  my heart is joyful because of your saving help.

6 I will sing to you, O LORD,
for you have dealt with me richly; *
I will praise the name of the Lord Most High.

14

1 Fools say in their heart, "There is no God." *
All are corrupt and commit abominable acts;
there is none who does any good.

2 The LORD looks down from heaven upon us all, *
to see if there is any who is wise,
if there is one who seeks after God.

3 Every one has proved faithless;
all alike have turned bad; *
there is none who does good; no, not one.

4 Have they no knowledge, all those evildoers *
who eat up my people like bread
and do not call upon the LORD?

5 See how they tremble with fear, *
because God is in the company of the righteous.

6 Their aim is to confound the plans of the afflicted, *
but the LORD is their refuge.

7 Oh, that Israel's deliverance would come out of Zion! *
when the LORD restores the fortunes of the chosen people,
Jacob will rejoice and Israel be glad.

15

1 LORD, who may dwell in your tabernacle? *
who may abide upon your holy hill?

2 Those who lead a blameless life and do what is right, *
who speak the truth from their heart.

3 There is no guile upon their tongue;
they do no evil to their friend; *
they do not heap contempt upon their neighbor.

4 In their sight the wicked are rejected, *
   but they honor those who fear the LORD.

5 They have sworn to do no wrong *
   and do not take back their word.

6 They do not give their money in hope of gain, *
   nor do they take a bribe against the innocent.

7 Those who do these things *
   shall never be overthrown.

16

1 Protect me, O God, for I take refuge in you; *
   I have said to the LORD, "You are my Lord,
   my good above all other."

2 All my delight is upon the godly that are in the land, *
   upon those who are noble among the people.

3 But those who run after other gods *
   shall have their troubles multiplied.

4 Their libations of blood I will not offer, *
   nor take the names of their gods upon my lips.

5 O LORD, you are my portion and my cup; *
   it is you who uphold my lot.

6 My boundaries enclose a pleasant land; *
   indeed, I have a goodly heritage.

7 I will bless the LORD who gives me counsel; *
   my heart teaches me, night after night.

8 I have set the LORD always before me; *
   because you are at my right hand I shall not fall.

9 My heart, therefore, is glad, and my spirit rejoices; *
   my body also shall rest in hope.

10 For you will not abandon me to the grave, *
   nor let your holy one see the pit.

11 You will show me the path of life; *
   in your presence there is fullness of joy,
   and in your right hand are pleasures for evermore.

17

1 Hear my plea of innocence, O LORD;
   give heed to my cry; *
   listen to my prayer, which does not come from lying lips.

2 Let my vindication come forth from your presence; *
   let your eyes be fixed on justice.

3 Weigh my heart, summon me by night, *
   melt me down; you will find no impurity in me.

4 I give no offense with my mouth as others do; *
   I have heeded the words of your lips.

5 My footsteps hold fast to the ways of your law; *
   in your paths my feet shall not stumble.

6 I call upon you, O God, for you will answer me; *
   incline your ear to me and hear my words.

7 Show me your marvelous loving-kindness, *
   O Savior of those who take refuge at your right hand
   from those who rise up against them.

8 Keep me as the apple of your eye; *
   hide me under the shadow of your wings,

9 From the wicked who assault me, *
   from my deadly enemies who surround me.

10 They have closed their heart to pity, *
   and their mouth speaks proud things.

11 They press me hard,
   now they surround me, *
   watching how they may cast me to the ground,

12 Like a lion, greedy for its prey, *
   and like a young lion lurking in secret places.

13 Arise, O Lord; confront them and bring them down; *
   deliver me from the wicked by your sword.

14 Deliver me, O Lord, by your hand *
   from those whose portion in life is this world;

15 Whose bellies you fill with your treasure, *
   who are well supplied with children
   and leave their wealth to their little ones.

16 But at my vindication I shall see your face; *
   when I awake, I shall be satisfied, beholding your likeness.

18

1 I love you, O Lord my strength, *
   O Lord my stronghold, my crag, and my haven.

2 My God, my rock in whom I put my trust, *
   my shield, the horn of my salvation, and my refuge;
   you are worthy of praise.

3 I will call upon the Lord, *
   and so shall I be saved from my enemies.

4 The breakers of death rolled over me, *
   and the torrents of oblivion made me afraid.

5 The cords of hell entangled me, *
   and the snares of death were set for me.

6 I called upon the Lord in my distress *
   and cried out to my God for help.

7 You heard my voice from your heavenly dwelling; *
   my cry of anguish came to your ears.

8 The earth reeled and rocked; *
   the roots of the mountains shook;
   they reeled because of your anger.

9 Smoke rose from your nostrils
   and a consuming fire out of your mouth; *
   hot burning coals blazed forth from you.

26

10 You parted the heavens and came down *
     with a storm cloud under your feet.

11 You mounted on cherubim and flew; *
     you swooped on the wings of the wind.

12 You wrapped darkness about you; *
     you made dark waters and thick clouds your pavilion.

13 From the brightness of your presence, through the clouds, *
     burst hailstones and coals of fire.

14 O LORD, you thundered out of heaven; *
     O Most High, you uttered your voice.

15 You loosed your arrows and scattered them; *
     you hurled thunderbolts and routed them.

16 The beds of the seas were uncovered,
     and the foundations of the world laid bare, *
       at your battle cry, O LORD,
       at the blast of the breath of your nostrils.

17 You reached down from on high and grasped me; *
     you drew me out of great waters.

18 You delivered me from my strong enemies
     and from those who hated me; *
       for they were too mighty for me.

19 They confronted me in the day of my disaster; *
     but the LORD was my support.

20 You brought me out into an open place; *
     you rescued me because you delighted in me.

21 The LORD rewarded me because of my righteous dealing; *
     because my hands were clean God rewarded me;

22 For I have kept the ways of the LORD *
     and have not offended against my God;

23 For all God's judgments are before my eyes, *
     and the decrees of the LORD I have not put away from me;

24 For I have been blameless with the LORD *
    and have kept myself from iniquity;

25 Therefore the LORD rewarded me according to my righteous dealing, *
    seeing the cleanness of my hands.

26 With the faithful you show yourself faithful, O God; *
    with the forthright you show yourself forthright.

27 With the pure you show yourself pure, *
    but with the crooked you are wily.

28 You will save a lowly people, *
    but you will humble the haughty eyes.

29 You, O LORD, are my lamp; *
    my God, you make my darkness bright.

30 With you I will break down an enclosure; *
    with the help of my God I will scale any wall.

31 As for you, O God, your ways are perfect;
    the words of the LORD are tried in the fire; *
    you are a shield to all who trust in you.

32 For who is God, but the LORD? *
    who is the Rock, except our God?

33 It is God who girds me about with strength *
    and makes my way secure.

34 You make me sure-footed like a deer *
    and let me stand firm on the heights.

35 You train my hands for battle *
    and my arms for bending even a bow of bronze.

36 You have given me your shield of victory; *
    your right hand also sustains me;
    your loving care makes me great.

37 You lengthen my stride beneath me, *
    and my ankles do not give way.

38 I pursue my enemies and overtake them; *
  I will not turn back till I have destroyed them.

39 I strike them down, and they cannot rise; *
  they fall defeated at my feet.

40 You have girded me with strength for the battle; *
  you have cast down my adversaries beneath me;
  you have put my enemies to flight.

41 I destroy those who hate me;
  they cry out, but there is none to help them; *
  they cry to the LORD, who does not answer.

42 I beat them small like dust before the wind; *
  I trample them like mud in the streets.

43 You deliver me from the strife of the peoples; *
  you put me at the head of the nations.

44 A people I have not known shall serve me;
  no sooner shall they hear than they shall obey me; *
  strangers will cringe before me.

45 The foreign peoples will lose heart; *
  they shall come trembling out of their strongholds.

46 The LORD lives! Blessed is my Rock! *
  Exalted is the God of my salvation!

47 The LORD is the God who gave me victory *
  and cast down the peoples beneath me.

48 You rescued me from the fury of my enemies;
  you exalted me above those who rose against me; *
  you saved me from my deadly foe.

49 Therefore will I extol you among the nations, O LORD, *
  and sing praises to your name.

50 You multiply the victories of your king; *
  you show loving-kindness to your anointed,
  to David and his descendants for ever.

19

1 The heavens declare the glory of God, *
and the firmament shows forth the work of God's hands.

2 One day tells its tale to another, *
and one night imparts knowledge to another.

3 Although they have no words or language, *
and their voices are not heard,

4 Their sound has gone out into all lands, *
and their message to the ends of the world.

5 In the deep has God set a pavilion for the sun; *
it comes forth like a bridegroom out of his chamber;
it rejoices like a champion to run its course.

6 It goes forth from the uttermost edge of the heavens
and runs about to the end of it again; *
nothing is hidden from its burning heat.

7 The law of the LORD is perfect and revives the soul; *
the testimony of the LORD is sure and gives wisdom to the
innocent.

8 The statutes of the LORD are just and rejoice the heart; *
the commandment of the LORD is clear and gives light to the eyes.

9 The fear of the LORD is clean and endures for ever; *
the judgments of the LORD are true and righteous altogether.

10 More to be desired are they than gold, more than much fine gold, *
sweeter far than honey, than honey in the comb.

11 By them also is your servant enlightened, *
and in keeping them there is great reward.

12 Can people tell how often they offend? *
cleanse me from my secret faults.

13 Above all, keep your servant from presumptuous sins;
let them not get dominion over me; *
then shall I be whole and sound,
and innocent of a great offense.

14 Let the words of my mouth and the meditation of my heart be
        acceptable in your sight, *
      O LORD, my strength and my redeemer.

20

1 May the LORD answer you in the day of trouble, *
      the name of the God of Jacob defend you.

2 From God's holy place may you receive help; *
      may God strengthen you out of Zion.

3 May God remember all your offerings *
      and accept your burnt sacrifice;

4 Grant you your heart's desire *
      and prosper all your plans.

5 We will shout for joy at your victory
   and triumph in the name of our God; *
      may the LORD grant all your requests.

6 Now I know that the LORD gives victory to the anointed one; *
      out of God's holy heaven will come an answer;
      the right hand of the LORD works victorious strength.

7 Some put their trust in chariots and some in horses, *
      but we will call upon the name of the LORD our God.

8 They collapse and fall down, *
      but we will arise and stand upright.

9 O LORD, give victory to the king *
      and answer us when we call.

21

1 The king rejoices in your strength, O LORD; *
      how greatly he exults in your victory!

2 You have given him his heart's desire; *
      you have not denied him the request of his lips.

3 For you meet him with blessings of prosperity, *
      and set a crown of fine gold upon his head.

4 He asked you for life, and you gave it to him: *
   length of days, for ever and ever.

5 His honor is great, because of your victory; *
   splendor and majesty have you bestowed upon him.

6 For you will give him everlasting felicity *
   and will make him glad with the joy of your presence.

7 For the king puts his trust in the LORD; *
   because of the loving-kindness of the Most High, he will not fall.

8 Your hand will lay hold upon all your enemies; *
   your right hand will seize all those who hate you.

9 You will make them like a fiery furnace *
   at the time of your appearing, O LORD;

10 You will swallow them up in your wrath, *
   and fire shall consume them.

11 You will destroy their offspring from the land *
   and their descendants from among the peoples of the earth.

12 Though they intend evil against you
and devise wicked schemes, *
   yet they shall not prevail.

13 For you will put them to flight *
   and aim your arrows at them.

14 Be exalted, O LORD, in your might; *
   we will sing and praise your power.

22

1 My God, my God, why have you forsaken me? *
   and are so far from my cry
   and from the words of my distress?

2 O my God, I cry in the daytime, but you do not answer; *
   by night as well, but I find no rest.

3 Yet you are the Holy One, *
   enthroned upon the praises of Israel.

4 Our ancestors put their trust in you; *
   they trusted, and you delivered them.

5 They cried out to you and were delivered; *
   they trusted in you and were not put to shame.

6 But as for me, I am a worm and not a man, *
   scorned by all and despised by the people.

7 All who see me laugh me to scorn; *
   they curl their lips and wag their heads, saying,

8 "He trusted in the LORD; let the LORD deliver him; *
   let God rescue him, if God delights in him."

9 Yet you are the one who took me out of the womb, *
   and kept me safe upon my mother's breast.

10 I have been entrusted to you ever since I was born; *
   you were my God when I was still in my mother's womb.

11 Be not far from me, for trouble is near, *
   and there is none to help.

12 Many young bulls encircle me; *
   strong bulls of Bashan surround me.

13 They open wide their jaws at me, *
   like a ravening and a roaring lion.

14 I am poured out like water;
   all my bones are out of joint; *
   my heart within my breast is melting wax.

15 My mouth is dried out like a pot-sherd;
   my tongue sticks to the roof of my mouth; *
   and you have laid me in the dust of the grave.

16 Packs of dogs close me in,
   and gangs of evildoers circle around me; *
   they pierce my hands and my feet;
   I can count all my bones.

17 They stare and gloat over me; *
    they divide my garments among them;
    they cast lots for my clothing.

18 Be not far away, O Lord; *
    you are my strength; hasten to help me.

19 Save me from the sword, *
    my life from the power of the dog.

20 Save me from the lion's mouth, *
    my wretched body from the horns of wild bulls.

21 I will declare your name to the community; *
    in the midst of the congregation I will praise you.

22 Praise the Lord, you that are God-fearing; *
    stand in awe of the Lord, O offspring of Israel;
    all you of Jacob's line, give glory.

23 For the Lord does not despise nor abhor the poor in their poverty;
    neither is the Lord's face hidden from them; *
    but when they cry out, the Lord hears them.

24 My praise is of God in the great assembly; *
    I will perform my vows in the presence of those who worship
      the Lord.

25 The poor shall eat and be satisfied,
    and those who seek the Lord shall give praise: *
    "May your heart live for ever!"

26 All the ends of the earth shall remember and turn to God, *
    and all the families of the nations
    shall bow before the Lord.

27 For sovereignty belongs to the Lord, *
    who rules over the nations.

28 To the Lord alone all who sleep in the earth bow down in
      worship; *
    all who go down to the dust fall before the Lord.

29 My soul shall live for God;
  my descendants shall serve the LORD; *
    they shall be known as the LORD's for ever.

30 They shall come and make known to a people yet unborn *
  the saving deeds that God has done.

23

1 The LORD is my shepherd; *
  I shall not be in want.

2 You make me lie down in green pastures *
  and lead me beside still waters.

3 You revive my soul *
  and guide me along right pathways for your name's sake.

4 Though I walk through the valley of the shadow of death,
  I shall fear no evil; *
    for you are with me;
    your rod and your staff, they comfort me.

5 You spread a table before me in the presence of those who
    trouble me; *
    you have anointed my head with oil,
    and my cup is running over.

6 Surely your goodness and mercy shall follow me all the days of
    my life, *
    and I will dwell in the house of the LORD for ever.

24

1 The earth is the LORD's and all that is in it, *
  the world and all who dwell therein.

2 For it is the LORD who founded it upon the seas *
  and made it firm upon the rivers of the deep.

3 "Who can ascend the hill of the LORD? *
  and who can stand in God's holy place?"

4 "Those who have clean hands and a pure heart, *
   who have not pledged themselves to falsehood,
   nor sworn by what is a fraud.

5 They shall receive a blessing from the LORD *
   and a just reward from the God of their salvation."

6 Such is the generation of those who seek the LORD, *
   of those who seek your face, O God of Jacob.

7 Lift up your heads, O gates;
   lift them high, O everlasting doors; *
   and the glorious Sovereign shall come in.

8 "Who is this glorious Sovereign?" *
   "The LORD, strong and mighty,
   the LORD, mighty in battle."

9 Lift up your heads, O gates;
   lift them high, O everlasting doors; *
   and the glorious Sovereign shall come in.

10 "And who is this glorious Sovereign?" *
   "The LORD,
   the LORD of hosts is the glorious Sovereign."

25

1 To you, O LORD, I lift up my soul;
   my God, I put my trust in you; *
   let me not be humiliated,
   nor let my enemies triumph over me.

2 Let none who look to you be put to shame; *
   let the treacherous be disappointed in their schemes.

3 Show me your ways, O LORD, *
   and teach me your paths.

4 Lead me in your truth and teach me, *
   for you are the God of my salvation;
   in you have I trusted all the day long.

5 Remember, O LORD, your compassion and love, *
   for they are from everlasting.

6 Remember not the sins of my youth and my transgressions; *
   remember me according to your love
   and for the sake of your goodness, O LORD.

7 Gracious and upright are you, O LORD; *
   therefore you teach sinners in your way.

8 You guide the humble in doing right *
   and teach your way to the lowly.

9 All your paths, O LORD, are love and faithfulness *
   to those who keep your covenant and your testimonies.

10 For your name's sake, O LORD, *
   forgive my sin, for it is great.

11 Who are they who fear the LORD? *
   the LORD will teach them the way that they should choose.

12 They shall dwell in prosperity, *
   and their offspring shall inherit the land.

13 The LORD is a friend to the God-fearing *
   and will show them the holy covenant.

14 My eyes are ever looking to the LORD, *
   who shall pluck my feet out of the net.

15 Turn to me and have pity on me, *
   for I am left alone and in misery.

16 The sorrows of my heart have increased; *
   bring me out of my troubles.

17 Look upon my adversity and misery *
   and forgive me all my sin.

18 Look upon my enemies, for they are many, *
   and they bear a violent hatred against me.

19 Protect my life and deliver me; *
   let me not be put to shame, for I have trusted in you.

20 Let integrity and uprightness preserve me, *
      for my hope has been in you.

21 Deliver Israel, O God, *
      out of all their troubles.

26

1 Give judgment for me, O LORD,
   for I have lived with integrity; *
      I have trusted in the LORD and have not faltered.

2 Test me, O LORD, and try me; *
      examine my heart and my mind.

3 For your love is before my eyes; *
      I have walked faithfully with you.

4 I have not sat with the worthless, *
      nor do I consort with the deceitful.

5 I have hated the company of evildoers; *
      I will not sit down with the wicked.

6 I will wash my hands in innocence, O LORD, *
      that I may go in procession round your altar,

7 Singing aloud a song of thanksgiving *
      and recounting all your wonderful deeds.

8 LORD, I love the house in which you dwell *
      and the place where your glory abides.

9 Do not sweep me away with sinners, *
      nor my life with those who thirst for blood,

10 Whose hands are full of evil plots, *
      and their right hand full of bribes.

11 As for me, I will live with integrity; *
      redeem me, O LORD, and have pity on me.

12 My foot stands on level ground; *
      in the full assembly I will bless the LORD.

27

1 The LORD is my light and my salvation;
   whom then shall I fear? *
      the LORD is the strength of my life;
      of whom then shall I be afraid?

2 When evildoers came upon me to eat up my flesh, *
      it was they, my foes and my adversaries, who stumbled and fell.

3 Though an army should encamp against me, *
      yet my heart shall not be afraid;

4 And though war should rise up against me, *
      yet will I put my trust in the LORD.

5 One thing have I asked of the LORD;
   one thing I seek; *
      that I may dwell in the house of the LORD all the days of my life;

6 To behold the fair beauty of the LORD, *
      to seek God in the temple.

7 For on the day of trouble the LORD shall shelter me in safety; *
      the LORD shall hide me in the secrecy of the holy place
      and set me high upon a rock.

8 Even now the LORD lifts up my head *
      above my enemies round about me.

9 Therefore I will offer in the holy place an oblation
   with sounds of great gladness; *
      I will sing and make music to the LORD.

10 Hearken to my voice, O LORD, when I call; *
      have mercy on me and answer me.

11 You speak in my heart and say, "Seek my face." *
      Your face, LORD, will I seek.

12 Hide not your face from me, *
      nor turn away your servant in displeasure.

13 You have been my helper;
   cast me not away; *
      do not forsake me, O God of my salvation.

14 Though my father and my mother forsake me, *
    the LORD will sustain me.

15 Show me your way, O LORD; *
    lead me on a level path, because of my enemies.

16 Deliver me not into the hand of my adversaries, *
    for false witnesses have risen up against me,
    and also those who speak malice.

17 What if I had not believed
    that I should see the goodness of the LORD *
    in the land of the living!

18 O tarry and await the LORD's pleasure;
    be strong, and the LORD shall comfort your heart; *
    wait patiently for the LORD.

28

1 O LORD, I call to you;
    my Rock, do not be deaf to my cry; *
    lest, if you do not hear me,
    I become like those who go down to the pit.

2 Hear the voice of my prayer when I cry out to you, *
    when I lift up my hands to your holy of holies.

3 Do not snatch me away with the wicked or with the evildoers, *
    who speak peaceably with their neighbors,
    while strife is in their hearts.

4 Repay them according to their deeds, *
    and according to the wickedness of their actions.

5 According to the work of their hands repay them, *
    and give them their just deserts.

6 O LORD, they have no understanding of your doings,
    nor of the works of your hands; *
    therefore you will break them down and not build them up.

7 Blessed is the LORD! *
    for you have heard the voice of my prayer.

8 The LORD is my strength and my shield; *
      my heart trusts in you, and I have been helped;

9 Therefore my heart dances for joy, *
      and in my song will I praise you.

10 You, O LORD, are the strength of your people, *
       a safe refuge for your anointed.

11 Save your people and bless your inheritance; *
       shepherd them and carry them for ever.

29

1 Ascribe to the LORD, you gods, *
      ascribe to the LORD glory and strength.

2 Ascribe to the LORD the glory that is due the holy name; *
      worship the LORD in the beauty of holiness.

3 The voice of the LORD is upon the waters;
   the God of glory thunders; *
      the LORD is upon the mighty waters.

4 The voice of the LORD is a powerful voice; *
      the voice of the LORD is a voice of splendor.

5 The voice of the LORD breaks the cedar trees; *
      the LORD breaks the cedars of Lebanon;

6 The LORD makes Lebanon skip like a calf, *
      and Mount Hermon like a young wild ox.

7 The voice of the LORD splits the flames of fire;
   the voice of the LORD shakes the wilderness; *
      the LORD shakes the wilderness of Kadesh.

8 The voice of the LORD makes the oak trees writhe *
      and strips the forests bare.

9 And in the temple of the LORD *
      all are crying, "Glory!"

10 The LORD sits enthroned above the flood; *
       the LORD sits enthroned as Sovereign for evermore.

11 The LORD shall give strength to the chosen people; *
   the LORD shall give the people the blessing of peace.

30

1 I will exalt you, O LORD,
   because you have lifted me up *
      and have not let my enemies triumph over me.

2 O LORD my God, I cried out to you, *
   and you restored me to health.

3 You brought me up, O LORD, from the dead; *
   you restored my life as I was going down to the grave.

4 Sing to the LORD, you faithful servants; *
   give thanks for the remembrance of God's holiness.

5 For God's wrath lasts but the twinkling of an eye, *
   God's favor endures for a lifetime.

6 Weeping may spend the night, *
   but joy comes in the morning.

7 While I felt secure, I said,
   "I shall never be disturbed. *
      You, LORD, with your favor, made me as strong as the
         mountains."

8 Then you hid your face, *
   and I was filled with fear.

9 I cried to you, O LORD; *
   I pleaded with the Lord, saying,

10 "What profit is there in my blood, if I go down to the pit? *
   will the dust praise you or declare your faithfulness?

11 Hear, O LORD, and have mercy upon me; *
   O LORD, be my helper."

12 You have turned my wailing into dancing; *
   you have put off my sack-cloth and clothed me with joy.

13 Therefore my heart sings to you without ceasing; *
   O Lord my God, I will give you thanks for ever.

31

1 In you, O Lord, have I taken refuge;
   let me never be put to shame; *
      deliver me in your righteousness.

2 Incline your ear to me; *
   make haste to deliver me.

3 Be my strong rock, a castle to keep me safe,
   for you are my crag and my stronghold; *
      for the sake of your name, lead me and guide me.

4 Take me out of the net that they have secretly set for me, *
   for you are my tower of strength.

5 Into your hands I commend my spirit, *
   for you have redeemed me,
      O Lord, O God of truth.

6 I hate those who cling to worthless idols, *
   and I put my trust in the Lord.

7 I will rejoice and be glad because of your mercy; *
   for you have seen my affliction;
      you know my distress.

8 You have not shut me up in the power of the enemy; *
   you have set my feet in an open place.

9 Have mercy on me, O Lord, for I am in trouble; *
   my eye is consumed with sorrow,
      and also my throat and my belly.

10 For my life is wasted with grief,
   and my years with sighing; *
      my strength fails me because of affliction,
      and my bones are consumed.

11 I have become a reproach to all my enemies and even to my
      neighbors,
   a dismay to those of my acquaintance; *
      when they see me in the street they avoid me.

12 I am forgotten, out of mind, as if I were dead; *
      I am as useless as a broken pot.

13 For I have heard the whispering of the crowd;
   fear is all around; *
      they put their heads together against me;
      they plot to take my life.

14 But as for me, I have trusted in you, O LORD. *
      I have said, "You are my God.

15 My times are in your hand; *
      rescue me from the hand of my enemies,
      and from those who persecute me.

16 Make your face to shine upon your servant, *
      and in your loving-kindness save me."

17 LORD, let me not be ashamed for having called upon you; *
      rather, let the wicked be put to shame;
      let them be silent in the grave.

18 Let the lying lips be silenced which speak against the righteous, *
      haughtily, disdainfully, and with contempt.

19 How great is your goodness, O LORD!
   which you have laid up for those who fear you; *
      which you have done in the sight of all
      for those who put their trust in you.

20 You hide them in the covert of your presence from those who
      slander them; *
   you keep them in your shelter from the strife of tongues.

21 Blessed be the LORD! *
      for you have shown me the wonders of your love in a besieged
      city.

22 Yet I said in my alarm,
"I have been cut off from the sight of your eyes." *
Nevertheless, you heard the sound of my entreaty
when I cried out to you.

23 Love the LORD, all you who are faithful; *
the LORD protects the pious,
but repays to the full those who act haughtily.

24 Be strong and let your heart take courage, *
all you who wait for the LORD.

32

1 Happy are they whose transgressions are forgiven, *
and whose sin is put away!

2 Happy are they to whom the LORD imputes no guilt, *
and in whose spirit there is no guile!

3 While I held my tongue, my bones withered away, *
because of my groaning all day long.

4 For your hand was heavy upon me day and night; *
my moisture was dried up as in the heat of summer.

5 Then I acknowledged my sin to you, *
and did not conceal my guilt.

6 I said, "I will confess my transgressions to the LORD." *
Then you forgave me the guilt of my sin.

7 Therefore all the faithful will make their prayers to you in time
of trouble; *
when the great waters overflow, they shall not reach them.

8 You are my hiding-place;
you preserve me from trouble; *
you surround me with shouts of deliverance.

9 "I will instruct you and teach you in the way that you should go; *
I will guide you with my eye.

10 Do not be like horse or mule, which have no understanding; *
   who must be fitted with bit and bridle,
   or else they will not stay near you."

11 Great are the tribulations of the wicked; *
   but mercy embraces those who trust in the LORD.

12 Be glad, you righteous, and rejoice in the LORD; *
   shout for joy, all who are true of heart.

33

1 Rejoice in the LORD, you righteous; *
   it is good for the just to sing praises.

2 Praise the LORD with the harp; *
   play upon the psaltery and lyre.

3 Sing for the LORD a new song; *
   sound a fanfare with all your skill upon the trumpet.

4 For your word, O LORD, is right, *
   and all your works are sure.

5 You love righteousness and justice; *
   your loving-kindness, O LORD, fills the whole earth.

6 By your word, O LORD, were the heavens made, *
   by the breath of your mouth all the heavenly hosts.

7 You gather up the waters of the ocean as in a water-skin *
   and store up the depths of the sea.

8 Let all the earth fear the LORD; *
   let all who dwell in the world stand in reverence.

9 For the LORD spoke, and it came to pass; *
   the LORD commanded, and it stood fast.

10 The LORD brings the will of the nations to naught *
   and thwarts the designs of the peoples.

11 But the LORD's will stands fast for ever, *
   and the designs of the LORD's heart from age to age.

12 Happy is the nation whose God is the LORD! *
happy the people you have chosen to be your own!

13 O LORD, you look down from heaven *
and behold all the people in the world.

14 From where you sit enthroned you turn your gaze *
on all who dwell on the earth.

15 You fashion all the hearts of them *
and understand all their works.

16 There is no ruler that can be saved by a mighty army; *
a warrior is not delivered by great strength.

17 The horse is a vain hope for deliverance; *
for all its strength it cannot save.

18 Behold, your eye, O LORD, is upon those who fear you, *
on those who wait upon your love,

19 To pluck their lives from death, *
and to feed them in time of famine.

20 Our soul waits for you, O LORD; *
you are our help and our shield.

21 Indeed, our heart rejoices in you, *
for in your holy name we put our trust.

22 Let your loving-kindness, O LORD, be upon us, *
as we have put our trust in you.

34

1 At all times I will bless the LORD, *
whose praise shall ever be in my mouth.

2 I will glory in the LORD; *
let the humble hear and rejoice.

3 Proclaim with me the greatness of the LORD; *
let us exalt the name of the LORD together.

4 I sought the LORD, who answered me *
and delivered me out of all my terror.

5 Look upon the LORD and be radiant, *
   and let not your faces be ashamed.

6 I called in my affliction and the LORD heard me *
   and saved me from all my troubles.

7 The angel of the LORD encompasses the God-fearing, *
   and the LORD will deliver them.

8 Taste and see that the LORD is good; *
   happy are they who trust in the LORD!

9 Fear the LORD, you holy ones, *
   for those who are God-fearing lack nothing.

10 The young lions lack and suffer hunger, *
    but those who seek the LORD lack nothing that is good.

11 Come, children, and listen to me; *
    I will teach you the fear of the LORD.

12 Who among you loves life *
    and desires long life to enjoy prosperity?

13 Keep your tongue from evil-speaking *
    and your lips from lying words.

14 Turn from evil and do good; *
    seek peace and pursue it.

15 The eyes of the LORD are upon the righteous, *
    and the ears of the LORD are open to their cry.

16 The face of the LORD is against those who do evil, *
    to root out the remembrance of them from the earth.

17 The righteous cry, and the LORD hears them *
    and delivers them from all their troubles.

18 The LORD is near to the brokenhearted *
    and will save those whose spirits are crushed.

19 Many are the troubles of the righteous, *
    but the LORD will deliver the just out of them all.

20 The LORD will keep safe the bones of the righteous; *
   not one of them shall be broken.

21 Evil shall slay the wicked, *
   and those who hate the righteous will be punished.

22 The LORD ransoms the life of those chosen to serve, *
   and none will be punished who trust in the LORD.

35

1 Fight those who fight me, O LORD; *
   attack those who are attacking me.

2 Take up shield and armor *
   and rise up to help me.

3 Draw the sword and bar the way against those who pursue me; *
   say to my soul, "I am your salvation."

4 Let those who seek after my life be shamed and humbled, *
   let those who plot my ruin fall back and be dismayed.

5 Let them be like chaff before the wind, *
   and let the angel of the LORD drive them away.

6 Let their way be dark and slippery, *
   and let the angel of the LORD pursue them.

7 For they have secretly spread a net for me without a cause; *
   without a cause they have dug a pit to take me alive.

8 Let ruin come upon them unawares; *
   let them be caught in the net they hid;
   let them fall into the pit they dug.

9 Then I will be joyful in you, O LORD; *
   I will glory in your victory.

10 My very bones will say, "LORD, who is like you? *
   You deliver the poor from those who are too strong for them,
   the poor and needy from those who rob them."

11 Malicious witnesses rise up against me; *
   they charge me with matters I know nothing about.

12 They pay me evil in exchange for good; *
   my soul is full of despair.

13 But when they were sick I dressed in sack-cloth *
   and humbled myself by fasting;

14 I prayed with my whole heart,
   as one would for a friend or a brother; *
      I behaved like one who mourns for a mother,
      bowed down and grieving.

15 But when I stumbled, they were glad and gathered together;
   they gathered against me; *
      strangers whom I did not know tore me to pieces and would
         not stop.

16 They put me to the test and mocked me; *
   they gnashed at me with their teeth.

17 O Lord, how long will you look on? *
   rescue me from the roaring beasts,
   and my life from the young lions.

18 I will give you thanks in the great congregation; *
   I will praise you in the mighty throng.

19 Do not let my treacherous foes rejoice over me, *
   nor let those who hate me without a cause wink at each other.

20 For they do not plan for peace, *
   but invent deceitful schemes against the quiet in the land.

21 They opened their mouths at me and said, *
   "Aha! we saw it with our own eyes."

22 You saw it, O Lord; do not be silent; *
   O Lord, be not far from me.

23 Awake, arise, to my cause! *
   to my defense, my God and my Lord!

24 Give me justice, O Lord my God,
   according to your righteousness; *
      do not let them triumph over me.

25 Do not let them say in their hearts,
 "Aha! just what we want!" *
 Do not let them say, "We have swallowed you up."

26 Let all who rejoice at my ruin be ashamed and disgraced; *
 let those who boast against me be clothed with dismay and
 shame.

27 Let those who favor my cause sing out with joy and be glad; *
 let them say always, "Great are you, O LORD;
 you desire the prosperity of your servant."

28 And my tongue shall be talking of your righteousness *
 and of your praise all the day long.

36

1 There is a voice of rebellion deep in the heart of the wicked; *
 there is no fear of God before their eyes.

2 They flatter themselves in their own eyes *
 that their hateful sin will not be found out.

3 The words of their mouth are wicked and deceitful; *
 they have left off acting wisely and doing good.

4 They think up wickedness upon their beds
 and have set themselves in no good way; *
 they do not abhor that which is evil.

5 Your love, O LORD, reaches to the heavens, *
 and your faithfulness to the clouds.

6 Your righteousness is like the strong mountains,
 your justice like the great deep; *
 you save humans and beasts alike, O LORD.

7 How priceless is your love, O God! *
 your people take refuge under the shadow of your wings.

8 They feast upon the abundance of your house; *
 you give them drink from the river of your delights.

9 For with you is the well of life, *
 and in your light we see light.

10 Continue your loving-kindness to those who know you, *
    and your favor to those who are true of heart.

11 Let not the foot of the proud come near me, *
    nor the hand of the wicked push me aside.

12 See how they are fallen, those who work wickedness! *
    they are cast down and shall not be able to rise.

37

1 Do not fret yourself because of evildoers; *
    do not be jealous of those who do wrong.

2 For they shall soon wither like the grass, *
    and like the green grass fade away.

3 Put your trust in the LORD and do good; *
    dwell in the land and feed on its riches.

4 Take delight in the LORD, *
    who shall give you your heart's desire.

5 Commit your way to the LORD; put your trust in the LORD, *
    who will bring it to pass.

6 The LORD will make your righteousness as clear as the light *
    and your just dealing as the noonday.

7 Be still before the LORD; *
    wait patiently for the LORD.

8 Do not fret yourself over the one who prospers, *
    the one who succeeds in evil schemes.

9 Refrain from anger, leave rage alone; *
    do not fret yourself; it leads only to evil.

10 For evildoers shall be cut off, *
    but those who wait upon the LORD shall possess the land.

11 In a little while the wicked shall be no more; *
    you shall search out their place, but they will not be there.

12 But the lowly shall possess the land; *
    they will delight in abundance of peace.

13 The wicked plot against the righteous *
   and gnash at them with their teeth.

14 The Lord laughs at the wicked, *
   knowing that their day will come.

15 The wicked draw their sword and bend their bow
   to strike down the poor and needy, *
   to slaughter those who are upright in their ways.

16 Their sword shall go through their own heart, *
   and their bow shall be broken.

17 The little that the righteous has *
   is better than great riches of the wicked.

18 For the power of the wicked shall be broken, *
   but the LORD upholds the righteous.

19 The LORD cares for the lives of the godly, *
   and their inheritance shall last for ever.

20 They shall not be ashamed in bad times, *
   and in days of famine they shall have enough.

21 As for the wicked, they shall perish, *
   and the enemies of the LORD, like the glory of the meadows,
      shall vanish;
   they shall vanish like smoke.

22 The wicked borrow and do not repay, *
   but the righteous are generous in giving.

23 Those who are blessed by God shall possess the land, *
   but those who are cursed shall be destroyed.

24 Our steps are directed by the LORD; *
   those in whose way God delights, God strengthens.

25 If they stumble, they shall not fall headlong, *
   for the LORD holds them by the hand.

26 I have been young and now I am old, *
   but never have I seen the righteous forsaken,
   or their children begging bread.

27 The righteous are always generous in their lending, *
    and their children shall be a blessing.

28 Turn from evil, and do good, *
    and dwell in the land for ever.

29 For the LORD loves justice *
    and does not forsake the faithful.

30 They shall be kept safe for ever, *
    but the offspring of the wicked shall be destroyed.

31 The righteous shall possess the land *
    and dwell in it for ever.

32 The mouth of the righteous utters wisdom, *
    and their tongue speaks what is right.

33 The law of their God is in their heart, *
    and their footsteps shall not falter.

34 The wicked spy on the righteous *
    and seek occasion to kill them.

35 The LORD will not abandon them to their hand, *
    nor let them be found guilty when brought to trial.

36 Wait upon the LORD and keep God's way; *
    the LORD will raise you up to possess the land,
    and when the wicked are cut off, you will see it.

37 I have seen the wicked in their arrogance, *
    flourishing like a tree in full leaf.

38 I went by, and behold, they were not there; *
    I searched for them, but they could not be found.

39 Mark those who are honest;
    observe the upright; *
    for there is a future for the peaceable.

40 Transgressors shall be destroyed, one and all; *
    the future of the wicked is cut off.

41 But the deliverance of the righteous comes from the LORD, *
    who is their stronghold in time of trouble.

42 The LORD will help them and rescue them; *
  the LORD will rescue them from the wicked and deliver them,
  because in the LORD they seek refuge.

38

1 O LORD, do not rebuke me in your anger; *
  do not punish me in your wrath.

2 For your arrows have already pierced me, *
  and your hand presses hard upon me.

3 There is no health in my flesh,
  because of your indignation; *
    there is no soundness in my body, because of my sin.

4 For my iniquities overwhelm me; *
  like a heavy burden they are too much for me to bear.

5 My wounds stink and fester *
  by reason of my foolishness.

6 I am utterly bowed down and prostrate; *
  I go about in mourning all the day long.

7 Searing pain fills my innards; *
  there is no health in my body.

8 I am utterly numb and crushed; *
  I wail, because of the groaning of my heart.

9 O Lord, you know all my desires, *
  and my sighing is not hidden from you.

10 My heart is pounding, my strength has failed me, *
  and the brightness of my eyes is gone from me.

11 My friends and companions draw back from my affliction; *
  my neighbors stand afar off.

12 Those who seek after my life lay snares for me; *
  those who strive to hurt me speak of my ruin
  and plot treachery all the day long.

13 But I am like the deaf who do not hear, *
    like those who are mute and do not open their mouth.

14 I have become like one who does not hear *
    and from whose mouth comes no defense.

15 For in you, O Lord, have I fixed my hope; *
    you will answer me, O Lord my God.

16 For I said, "Do not let them rejoice at my expense, *
    those who gloat over me when my foot slips."

17 Truly, I am on the verge of falling, *
    and my pain is always with me.

18 I will confess my iniquity *
    and be sorry for my sin.

19 Those who are my enemies without cause are mighty, *
    and many in number are those who wrongfully hate me.

20 Those who repay evil for good slander me, *
    because I follow the course that is right.

21 O Lord, do not forsake me; *
    be not far from me, O my God.

22 Make haste to help me, *
    O Lord of my salvation.

39

1 I said, "I will keep watch upon my ways, *
    so that I do not offend with my tongue.

2 I will put a muzzle on my mouth *
    while the wicked are in my presence."

3 So I held my tongue and said nothing; *
    I refrained from rash words;
    but my pain became unbearable.

4 My heart was hot within me;
    while I pondered, the fire burst into flame; *
    I spoke out with my tongue:

5 LORD, let me know my end and the number of my days, *
   so that I may know how short my life is.

6 You have given me a mere handful of days,
   and my lifetime is as nothing in your sight; *
      truly, even those who stand erect are but a puff of wind.

7 We walk about like a shadow,
   and in vain we are in turmoil; *
      we heap up riches and cannot tell who will gather them.

8 And now, what is my hope? *
   O Lord, my hope is in you.

9 Deliver me from all my transgressions *
   and do not make me the taunt of the fool.

10 I fell silent and did not open my mouth, *
   for surely it was you that did it.

11 Take your affliction from me; *
   I am worn down by the blows of your hand.

12 With rebukes for sin you punish us;
   like a moth you eat away all that is dear to us; *
      truly, everyone is but a puff of wind.

13 Hear my prayer, O LORD,
   and give ear to my cry; *
      hold not your peace at my tears.

14 For I am but a sojourner with you, *
   a wayfarer, as all my ancestors were.

15 Turn your gaze from me, that I may be glad again, *
   before I go my way and am no more.

40

1 I waited patiently upon you, O LORD; *
   you stooped to me and heard my cry.

2 You lifted me out of the desolate pit, out of the mire and clay; *
   you set my feet upon a high cliff and made my footing sure.

3 You put a new song in my mouth,
  a song of praise to our God; *
    many shall see, and stand in awe,
    and put their trust in the LORD.

4 Happy are they who trust in the LORD! *
    they do not resort to evil spirits or turn to false gods.

5 Great things are they that you have done, O LORD my God!
  how great your wonders and your plans for us! *
    there is none who can be compared with you.

6 Oh, that I could make them known and tell them! *
    but they are more than I can count.

7 In sacrifice and offering you take no pleasure *
    (you have given me ears to hear you);

8 Burnt-offering and sin-offering you have not required, *
    and so I said, "Behold, I come.

9 In the roll of the book it is written concerning me: *
    'I love to do your will, O my God;
    your law is deep in my heart.'"

10 I proclaimed righteousness in the great congregation; *
    behold, I did not restrain my lips;
    and that, O LORD, you know.

11 Your righteousness have I not hidden in my heart;
   I have spoken of your faithfulness and your deliverance; *
    I have not concealed your love and faithfulness from the great
      congregation.

12 You are the LORD;
   do not withhold your compassion from me; *
    let your love and your faithfulness keep me safe for ever,

13 For innumerable troubles have crowded upon me;
   my sins have overtaken me, and I cannot see; *
    they are more in number than the hairs of my head,
    and my heart fails me.

14 Be pleased, O LORD, to deliver me; *
   O Lord, make haste to help me.

15 Let them be ashamed and altogether dismayed
   who seek after my life to destroy it; *
      let them draw back and be disgraced
      who take pleasure in my misfortune.

16 Let those who say "Aha!" and gloat over me be confounded, *
   because they are ashamed.

17 Let all who seek you rejoice in you and be glad; *
   let those who love your salvation continually say,
   "Great is the LORD!"

18 Though I am poor and afflicted, *
   the Lord will have regard for me.

19 You are my helper and my deliverer; *
   do not tarry, O my God.

41

1 Happy are they who consider the poor and needy! *
   the LORD will deliver them in the time of trouble.

2 The LORD preserves them and keeps them alive,
   so that they may be happy in the land; *
      the LORD does not hand them over to the will of their enemies.

3 The LORD sustains them on their sickbed *
   and ministers to them in their illness.

4 I said, "LORD, be merciful to me; *
   heal me, for I have sinned against you."

5 My enemies are saying wicked things about me, *
   asking when I will die, and when my name will perish.

6 Even if they come to see me, they speak empty words; *
   their heart collects false rumors;
   they go outside and spread them.

7 All my enemies whisper together about me *
   and devise evil against me.

8 They say that a deadly thing has fastened on me, *
   that I have taken to my bed and will never get up again.

9 Even my best friend, whom I trusted,
   who broke bread with me, *
      has scorned me and turned against me.

10 But you, O LORD, be merciful to me and raise me up, *
   and I shall repay them.

11 By this I know you are pleased with me, *
   that my enemy does not triumph over me.

12 In my integrity you hold me fast, *
   and shall set me before your face for ever.

13 Blessed be the LORD God of Israel, *
   from age to age. Amen. Amen.

42

1 As the deer longs for the water-brooks, *
   so longs my soul for you, O God.

2 My soul is athirst for God, athirst for the living God; *
   when shall I come to appear before the presence of God?

3 My tears have been my food day and night, *
   while all day long they say to me,
   "Where now is your God?"

4 I pour out my soul when I think on these things: *
   how I went with the multitude and led them into the house
      of God,

5 With the voice of praise and thanksgiving, *
   among those who keep holy-day.

6 Why are you so full of heaviness, O my soul? *
   and why are you so disquieted within me?

7 Put your trust in God; *
   for I will yet give thanks to the One
   who is the help of my countenance, and my God.

8 My soul is heavy within me; *
        therefore I will remember you from the land of Jordan,
        and from the peak of Mizar among the heights of Hermon.

9 One deep calls to another in the noise of your cataracts; *
        all your rapids and floods have gone over me.

10 The LORD grants loving-kindness in the daytime; *
        in the night season the song of the LORD is with me,
        a prayer to the God of my life.

11 I will say to the God of my strength,
        "Why have you forgotten me? *
        and why do I go so heavily while the enemy oppresses me?"

12 While my bones are being broken, *
        my enemies mock me to my face;

13 All day long they mock me *
        and say to me, "Where now is your God?"

14 Why are you so full of heaviness, O my soul? *
        and why are you so disquieted within me?

15 Put your trust in God; *
        for I will yet give thanks to the One
        who is the help of my countenance, and my God.

43

1 Give judgment for me, O God,
        and defend my cause against an ungodly people; *
        deliver me from the deceitful and the wicked.

2 For you are the God of my strength;
        why have you put me from you? *
        and why do I go so heavily while the enemy oppresses me?

3 Send out your light and your truth, that they may lead me, *
        and bring me to your holy hill
        and to your dwelling;

4 That I may go to the altar of God,
to the God of my joy and gladness; *
and on the harp I will give thanks to you, O God my God.

5 Why are you so full of heaviness, O my soul? *
and why are you so disquieted within me?

6 Put your trust in God; *
for I will yet give thanks to the One
who is the help of my countenance, and my God.

44

1 We have heard with our ears, O God,
our ancestors have told us, *
the deeds you did in their days,
in the days of old.

2 How with your hand you drove the peoples out
and planted our ancestors in the land; *
how you destroyed nations and made your people flourish.

3 For they did not take the land by their sword,
nor did their arm win the victory for them, *
but your right hand, your arm, and the light of your
countenance,
because you favored them.

4 You are my Sovereign and my God; *
you command victories for Jacob.

5 Through you we pushed back our adversaries; *
through your name we trampled on those who rose up
against us.

6 For I do not rely on my bow, *
and my sword does not give me the victory.

7 Surely, you gave us victory over our adversaries *
and put those who hate us to shame.

8 Every day we gloried in God, *
and we will praise your name for ever.

9 Nevertheless, you have rejected and humbled us *
  and do not go forth with our armies.

10 You have made us fall back before our adversary, *
   and our enemies have plundered us.

11 You have made us like sheep to be eaten *
   and have scattered us among the nations.

12 You are selling your people for a trifle *
   and are making no profit on the sale of them.

13 You have made us the scorn of our neighbors, *
   a mockery and derision to those around us.

14 You have made us a byword among the nations, *
   a laughing-stock among the peoples.

15 My humiliation is daily before me, *
   and shame has covered my face;

16 Because of the taunts of the mockers and blasphemers, *
   because of the enemy and avenger.

17 All this has come upon us; *
   yet we have not forgotten you,
   nor have we betrayed your covenant.

18 Our heart never turned back, *
   nor did our footsteps stray from your path;

19 Though you thrust us down into a place of misery, *
   and covered us over with deep darkness.

20 If we have forgotten the name of our God, *
   or stretched out our hands to some strange god,

21 Will not God find it out? *
   for you know the secrets of the heart.

22 Indeed, for your sake we are killed all the day long; *
   we are accounted as sheep for the slaughter.

23 Awake, O Lord! why are you sleeping? *
   Arise! do not reject us for ever.

24 Why have you hidden your face *
   and forgotten our affliction and oppression?

25 We sink down into the dust; *
   our body cleaves to the ground.

26 Rise up, and help us, *
   and save us, for the sake of your steadfast love.

45

1 My heart is stirring with a noble song;
   let me recite what I have fashioned for the king; *
   my tongue shall be the pen of a skilled writer.

2 You are the fairest of men; *
   grace flows from your lips,
   because God has blessed you for ever.

3 Strap your sword upon your thigh, O mighty warrior, *
   in your pride and in your majesty.

4 Ride out and conquer in the cause of truth *
   and for the sake of justice.

5 Your right hand will show you marvelous things; *
   your arrows are very sharp, O mighty warrior.

6 The peoples are falling at your feet, *
   and the king's enemies are losing heart.

7 Your throne, O God, endures for ever and ever, *
   a scepter of righteousness is the scepter of your reign;
   you love righteousness and hate iniquity.

8 Therefore God, your God, has anointed you *
   with the oil of gladness above your fellows.

9 All your garments are fragrant with myrrh, aloes, and cassia, *
   and the music of strings from ivory palaces makes you glad.

10 Kings' daughters stand among the noble women of the court; *
   on your right hand is the queen,
   adorned with the gold of Ophir.

11 "Hear, O daughter; consider and listen closely; *
  forget your people and your father's house.

12 The king will have pleasure in your beauty; *
  he is your master; therefore do him honor.

13 The people of Tyre are here with a gift; *
  the rich among the people seek your favor."

14 All glorious is the princess as she enters; *
  her gown is cloth-of-gold.

15 In embroidered apparel she is brought to the king; *
  after her the bridesmaids follow in procession.

16 With joy and gladness they are brought, *
  and enter into the palace of the king.

17 "In place of fathers, O king, you shall have sons; *
  you shall make them princes over all the earth.

18 I will make your name to be remembered
  from one generation to another; *
    therefore nations will praise you for ever and ever."

46

1 God is our refuge and strength, *
  a very present help in trouble.

2 Therefore we will not fear, though the earth be moved, *
  and though the mountains be toppled into the depths of the sea;

3 Though its waters rage and foam, *
  and though the mountains tremble at its tumult.

4 The LORD of hosts is with us; *
  the God of Jacob is our stronghold.

5 There is a river whose streams make glad the city of God, *
  the holy habitation of the Most High.

6 God is in the midst of the city;
  it shall not be overthrown; *
    God shall help it at the break of day.

7 The nations make much ado, and the realms are shaken; *
    God has spoken, and the earth shall melt away.

8 The LORD of hosts is with us; *
    the God of Jacob is our stronghold.

9 Come now and look upon the works of the LORD, *
    what awesome things God has done on earth.

10 It is the LORD who makes war to cease in all the world, *
     who breaks the bow, and shatters the spear,
     and burns the shields with fire.

11 "Be still, then, and know that I am God; *
     I will be exalted among the nations;
     I will be exalted in the earth."

12 The LORD of hosts is with us; *
     the God of Jacob is our stronghold.

47

1 Clap your hands, all you peoples; *
    shout to God with a cry of joy.

2 For the LORD Most High is to be feared, *
    the great Sovereign over all the earth.

3 The LORD subdues the peoples under us, *
    and the nations under our feet.

4 The LORD chooses our inheritance for us, *
    the pride of the beloved Jacob.

5 God has gone up with a shout, *
    the LORD with the sound of the ram's-horn.

6 Sing praises to God, sing praises; *
    sing praises to our Sovereign, sing praises.

7 For God is Sovereign of all the earth; *
    sing praises with all your skill.

8 God reigns over the nations; *
    God sits upon heaven's holy throne.

9 The nobles of the peoples have gathered together *
   with the people of the God of Abraham.

10 The rulers of the earth belong to God, *
   and God is highly exalted.

48

1 Great is the LORD, and highly to be praised; *
   in the city of our God is the LORD's holy hill.

2 Beautiful and lofty, the joy of all the earth, is the hill of Zion, *
   the city of the great Sovereign and the very center of the world.

3 God is in the citadels of Zion; *
   God is known to be its sure refuge.

4 Behold, the rulers of the earth assembled *
   and marched forward together.

5 They looked and were astounded; *
   they retreated and fled in terror.

6 Trembling seized them there; *
   they writhed like a woman in childbirth,
   like ships of the sea when the east wind shatters them.

7 As we have heard, so have we seen,
   in the city of the LORD of hosts, in the city of our God; *
   God has established it for ever.

8 We have waited in silence on your loving-kindness, O God, *
   in the midst of your temple.

9 Your praise, like your name, O God, reaches to the world's end; *
   your right hand is full of justice.

10 Let Mount Zion be glad
   and the cities of Judah rejoice, *
   because of your judgments.

11 Make the circuit of Zion;
   walk round about it; *
   count the number of its towers.

12 Consider well its bulwarks;
     examine its strongholds; *
        that you may tell those who come after.

13 This God is our God for ever and ever; *
        God shall be our guide for evermore.

49

1 Hear this, all you peoples;
    hearken, all you who dwell in the world, *
        you of high degree and low, rich and poor together.

2 My mouth shall speak of wisdom, *
        and my heart shall meditate on understanding.

3 I will incline my ear to a proverb *
        and set forth my riddle upon the harp.

4 Why should I be afraid in evil days, *
        when the wickedness of those at my heels surrounds me,

5 The wickedness of those who put their trust in their goods, *
        and boast of their great riches?

6 We can never ransom ourselves, *
        or deliver to God the price of our life;

7 For the ransom of our life is so great, *
        that we should never have enough to pay it,

8 In order to live for ever and ever, *
        and never see the grave.

9 For we see that the wise die also;
    like the dull and stupid they perish *
        and leave their wealth to those who come after them.

10 Their graves shall be their homes for ever,
     their dwelling places from generation to generation, *
        though they call the lands after their own names.

11 Even though honored, they cannot live for ever; *
        they are like the beasts that perish.

12 Such is the way of those who foolishly trust in themselves, *
and the end of those who delight in their own words.

13 Like a flock of sheep they are destined to die;
death is their shepherd; *
they go down straightway to the grave.

14 Their form shall waste away, *
and the land of the dead shall be their home.

15 But God will ransom my life *
and snatch me from the grasp of death.

16 Do not be envious when some become rich, *
or when the grandeur of their house increases;

17 For they will carry nothing away at their death, *
nor will their grandeur follow them.

18 Though they thought highly of themselves while they lived, *
and were praised for their success,

19 They shall join the company of their ancestors, *
who will never see the light again.

20 Those who are honored, but have no understanding, *
are like the beasts that perish.

50

1 The LORD, the God of gods, has spoken *
and has called the earth from the rising of the sun to its setting.

2 Out of Zion, perfect in its beauty, *
God shines forth in glory.

3 Our God will come and will not keep silence; *
before God there is a consuming flame,
and round about a raging storm.

4 God calls the heavens and the earth from above *
to witness the judgment of the chosen people.

5 "Gather before me my loyal followers, *
   those who have made a covenant with me
   and sealed it with sacrifice."

6 Let the heavens declare the rightness of God's cause; *
   for it is God who is judge.

7 Hear, O my people, and I will speak:
   "O Israel, I will bear witness against you; *
   for I am God, your God.

8 I do not accuse you because of your sacrifices; *
   your offerings are always before me.

9 I will take no bull-calf from your stalls, *
   nor he-goats out of your pens;

10 For all the beasts of the forest are mine, *
   the herds in their thousands upon the hills.

11 I know every bird in the sky, *
   and the creatures of the fields are in my sight.

12 If I were hungry, I would not tell you, *
   for the whole world is mine and all that is in it.

13 Do you think I eat the flesh of bulls, *
   or drink the blood of goats?

14 Offer to God a sacrifice of thanksgiving *
   and make good your vows to the Most High.

15 Call upon me in the day of trouble; *
   I will deliver you, and you shall honor me."

16 But to the wicked God says: *
   "Why do you recite my statutes,
   and take my covenant upon your lips;

17 Since you refuse discipline, *
   and toss my words behind your back?

18 When you see thieves, you make them your friends, *
   and you cast in your lot with adulterers.

19 You have loosed your lips for evil, *
   and harnessed your tongue to a lie.

20 You are always speaking evil of your kin *
   and slandering your own flesh and blood.

21 These things you have done, and I kept still, *
   and you thought that I am like you.

22 I have made my accusation; *
   I have put my case in order before your eyes.

23 Consider this well, you who forget God, *
   lest I rend you and there be none to deliver you.

24 Whoever offers me the sacrifice of thanksgiving honors me; *
   but to those who keep in my way will I show the salvation
   of God."

51

1 Have mercy on me, O God, according to your loving-kindness; *
   in your great compassion blot out my offenses.

2 Wash me through and through from my wickedness *
   and cleanse me from my sin.

3 For I know my transgressions, *
   and my sin is ever before me.

4 Against you only have I sinned *
   and done what is evil in your sight.

5 And so you are justified when you speak *
   and upright in your judgment.

6 Indeed, I have been wicked from my birth, *
   a sinner from my mother's womb.

7 For behold, you look for truth deep within me, *
   and will make me understand wisdom secretly.

8 Purge me from my sin, and I shall be pure; *
   wash me, and I shall be clean indeed.

9 Make me hear of joy and gladness, *
   that the body you have broken may rejoice.

10 Hide your face from my sins *
    and blot out all my iniquities.

11 Create in me a clean heart, O God, *
    and renew a right spirit within me.

12 Cast me not away from your presence *
    and take not your holy Spirit from me.

13 Give me the joy of your saving help again *
    and sustain me with your bountiful Spirit.

14 I shall teach your ways to the wicked, *
    and sinners shall return to you.

15 Deliver me from death, O God, *
    and my tongue shall sing of your righteousness,
    O God of my salvation.

16 Open my lips, O Lord, *
    and my mouth shall proclaim your praise.

17 Had you desired it, I would have offered sacrifice, *
    but you take no delight in burnt-offerings.

18 The sacrifice of God is a troubled spirit; *
    a broken and contrite heart, O God, you will not despise.

19 Be favorable and gracious to Zion, *
    and rebuild the walls of Jerusalem.

20 Then you will be pleased with the appointed sacrifices,
    with burnt-offerings and oblations; *
    then shall they offer young bullocks upon your altar.

52

1 You tyrant, why do you boast of wickedness *
   against the godly all day long?

2 You plot ruin;
   your tongue is like a sharpened razor, *
      O worker of deception.

3 You love evil more than good *
   and lying more than speaking the truth.

4 You love all words that hurt, *
   O you deceitful tongue.

5 Oh, that God would demolish you utterly, *
   topple you, and snatch you from your dwelling,
   and root you out of the land of the living!

6 The righteous shall see and tremble, *
   and they shall laugh at you, saying,

7 "This is the one who did not take God for a refuge, *
   but trusted in great wealth
   and relied upon wickedness."

8 But I am like a green olive tree in the house of God; *
   I trust in the mercy of God for ever and ever.

9 I will give you thanks for what you have done *
   and declare the goodness of your name in the presence of
      the godly.

53

1 Fools say in their heart, "There is no God." *
   All are corrupt and commit abominable acts;
   there is none who does any good.

2 God looks down from heaven upon us all, *
   to see if there is any who is wise,
   if there is one who seeks after God.

3 Every one has proved faithless;
   all alike have turned bad; *
      there is none who does good; no, not one.

4 Have they no knowledge, those evildoers *
   who eat up my people like bread
   and do not call upon God?

5 See how greatly they tremble,
   such trembling as never was; *
       for God has scattered the bones of the enemy;
       they are put to shame, because God has rejected them.

6 Oh, that Israel's deliverance would come out of Zion! *
   when God restores the fortunes of the chosen people
   Jacob will rejoice and Israel be glad.

54

1 Save me, O God, by your name; *
   in your might, defend my cause.

2 Hear my prayer, O God; *
   give ear to the words of my mouth.

3 For the arrogant have risen up against me,
   and the ruthless have sought my life, *
       those who have no regard for God.

4 Behold, God is my helper; *
   it is the Lord who sustains my life.

5 Render evil to those who spy on me; *
   in your faithfulness, destroy them.

6 I will offer you a freewill sacrifice *
   and praise your name, O LORD, for it is good.

7 For you have rescued me from every trouble, *
   and my eye has seen the ruin of my foes.

55

1 Hear my prayer, O God; *
   do not hide yourself from my petition.

2 Listen to me and answer me; *
   I have no peace, because of my cares.

3 I am shaken by the noise of the enemy *
  and by the pressure of the wicked;

4 For they have cast an evil spell upon me *
  and are set against me in fury.

5 My heart quakes within me, *
  and the terrors of death have fallen upon me.

6 Fear and trembling have come over me, *
  and horror overwhelms me.

7 And I said, "Oh, that I had wings like a dove! *
  I would fly away and be at rest.

8 I would flee to a far-off place *
  and make my lodging in the wilderness.

9 I would hasten to escape *
  from the stormy wind and tempest."

10 Swallow them up, O Lord;
  confound their speech; *
    for I have seen violence and strife in the city.

11 Day and night the sentries make their rounds upon its walls, *
  but trouble and misery are in the midst of it.

12 There is corruption at its heart; *
  its streets are never free of oppression and deceit.

13 For had it been an adversary who taunted me,
  then I could have borne it; *
    or had it been enemies who vaunted themselves against me,
    then I could have hidden from them.

14 But it was you, my companion, *
  my own familiar friend, dear to my own heart.

15 We took sweet counsel together, *
  and walked with the throng in the house of God.

16 Let death come upon them suddenly;
  let them go down alive into the grave; *
    for wickedness is in their dwellings, in their very midst.

17 But I will call upon God, *
        and the LORD will deliver me.

18 In the evening, in the morning, and at noonday,
    I will complain and lament, *
        and the LORD will hear my voice.

19 God will bring me safely back from the battle waged against me; *
        for there are many who fight me.

20 God, who is enthroned of old, will hear me and bring them
            down; *
        they never change; they do not fear God.

21 My companion stretched forth a hand against a comrade *
        and broke a covenant.

22 The speech of my companion is softer than butter, *
        but with war at heart.

23 The words of my comrade are smoother than oil, *
        but they are drawn swords.

24 Cast your burden upon the LORD,
    who will sustain you; *
        the LORD will never let the righteous stumble.

25 For you will bring the bloodthirsty and deceitful *
        down to the pit of destruction, O God.

26 They shall not live out half their days, *
        but I will put my trust in you.

56

1 Have mercy on me, O God,
    for my enemies are hounding me; *
        all day long they assault and oppress me.

2 They hound me all the day long; *
        truly there are many who fight against me, O Most High.

3 Whenever I am afraid, *
        I will put my trust in you.

4 In God, whose word I praise,
   in God I trust and will not be afraid, *
     for what can flesh do to me?

5 All day long they damage my cause; *
   their only thought is to do me evil.

6 They band together; they lie in wait; *
   they spy upon my footsteps;
   because they seek my life.

7 Shall they escape despite their wickedness? *
   O God, in your anger, cast down the peoples.

8 You have noted my lamentation;
   put my tears into your bottle; *
     are they not recorded in your book?

9 Whenever I call upon you, my enemies will be put to flight; *
   this I know, for God is on my side.

10 In God the LORD, whose word I praise,
   in God I trust and will not be afraid, *
     for what can mortals do to me?

11 I am bound by the vow I made to you, O God; *
   I will present to you thank-offerings;

12 For you have rescued my soul from death and my feet from
    stumbling, *
   that I may walk before God in the light of the living.

57

1 Be merciful to me, O God, be merciful,
   for I have taken refuge in you; *
     in the shadow of your wings will I take refuge
     until this time of trouble has gone by.

2 I will call upon you, O Most High God, *
   the God who maintains my cause.

3 You will send from heaven and save me;
   you will confound those who trample upon me; *
      O God, you will send forth your love and your faithfulness.

4 I lie in the midst of lions that devour the people; *
      their teeth are spears and arrows,
      their tongue a sharp sword.

5 They have laid a net for my feet,
   and I am bowed low; *
      they have dug a pit before me,
      but have fallen into it themselves.

6 Exalt yourself above the heavens, O God, *
      and your glory over all the earth.

7 My heart is firmly fixed, O God, my heart is fixed; *
      I will sing and make melody.

8 Wake up, my spirit;
   awake, lute and harp; *
      I myself will waken the dawn.

9 I will confess you among the peoples, O LORD; *
      I will sing praise to you among the nations.

10 For your loving-kindness is greater than the heavens, *
      and your faithfulness reaches to the clouds.

11 Exalt yourself above the heavens, O God, *
      and your glory over all the earth.

58

1 Do you indeed decree righteousness, you rulers? *
      do you judge the peoples with equity?

2 No; you devise evil in your hearts, *
      and your hands deal out violence in the land.

3 The wicked are perverse from the womb; *
      liars go astray from their birth.

4 They are as venomous as a serpent, *
      they are like the deaf adder which stops its ears,

5 Which does not heed the voice of the charmer, *
   no matter how skillful the charming.

6 O God, break their teeth in their mouths; *
   pull the fangs of the young lions, O LORD.

7 Let them vanish like water that runs off; *
   let them wither like trodden grass.

8 Let them be like the snail that melts away, *
   like a stillborn child that never sees the sun.

9 Before they bear fruit, let them be cut down like a brier; *
   like thorns and thistles let them be swept away.

10 The righteous will be glad when they see the vengeance; *
    they will bathe their feet in the blood of the wicked.

11 And they will say,
    "Surely, there is a reward for the righteous; *
    surely, there is a God who rules in the earth."

59

1 Rescue me from my enemies, O God; *
   protect me from those who rise up against me.

2 Rescue me from evildoers *
   and save me from those who thirst for my blood.

3 See how they lie in wait for my life,
   how the mighty gather together against me; *
   not for any offense or fault of mine, O LORD.

4 Not because of any guilt of mine *
   they run and prepare themselves for battle.

5 Rouse yourself, come to my side, and see; *
   for you, LORD God of hosts, are Israel's God.

6 Awake, and punish all the ungodly; *
   show no mercy to those who are faithless and evil.

7 They go to and fro in the evening; *
   they snarl like dogs and run about the city.

8 Behold, they boast with their mouths,
and taunts are on their lips; *
    "For who," they say, "will hear us?"

9 But you, O LORD, you laugh at them; *
    you laugh all the ungodly to scorn.

10 My eyes are fixed on you, O my Strength; *
    for you, O God, are my stronghold.

11 My merciful God comes to meet me; *
    God will let me look in triumph on my enemies.

12 Slay them, O God, lest my people forget; *
    send them reeling by your might
    and put them down, O Lord our shield.

13 For the sins of their mouths, for the words of their lips,
for the cursing and lies that they utter, *
    let them be caught in their pride.

14 Make an end of them in your wrath; *
    make an end of them, and they shall be no more.

15 Let everyone know that God rules in Jacob, *
    and to the ends of the earth.

16 They go to and fro in the evening; *
    they snarl like dogs and run about the city.

17 They forage for food, *
    and if they are not filled, they howl.

18 For my part, I will sing of your strength; *
    I will celebrate your love in the morning;

19 For you have become my stronghold, *
    a refuge in the day of my trouble.

20 To you, O my Strength, will I sing; *
    for you, O God, are my stronghold and my merciful God.

60

1 O God, you have cast us off and broken us; *
you have been angry;
oh, take us back to you again.

2 You have shaken the earth and split it open; *
repair the cracks in it, for it totters.

3 You have made your people know hardship; *
you have given us wine that makes us stagger.

4 You have set up a banner for those who fear you, *
to be a refuge from the power of the bow.

5 Save us by your right hand and answer us, *
that those who are dear to you may be delivered.

6 From God's holy place came a voice; *
God said, "I will exult and parcel out Shechem;
I will divide the valley of Succoth.

7 Gilead is mine and Manasseh is mine; *
Ephraim is my helmet and Judah my scepter.

8 Moab is my wash-basin,
on Edom I throw down my sandal to claim it, *
and over Philistia will I shout in triumph."

9 Who will lead me into the strong city? *
who will bring me into Edom?

10 Have you not cast us off, O God? *
you no longer go out, O God, with our armies.

11 Grant us your help against the enemy, *
for vain is the help of mortals.

12 With God we will do valiant deeds, *
and God shall tread our enemies under foot.

61

1 Hear my cry, O God, *
and listen to my prayer.

2 I call upon you from the ends of the earth
with heaviness in my heart; *
  set me upon the rock that is higher than I.

3 For you have been my refuge, *
  a strong tower against the enemy.

4 I will dwell in your house for ever; *
  I will take refuge under the cover of your wings.

5 For you, O God, have heard my vows; *
  you have granted me the heritage of those who fear your name.

6 Add length of days to our ruler's life, *
  with years extending over many generations.

7 Let our ruler sit enthroned before God for ever, *
  watched over by your love and faithfulness.

8 So will I always sing the praise of your name, *
  and day by day I will fulfill my vows.

62

1 For God alone my soul in silence waits; *
  from God comes my salvation.

2 God alone is my rock and my salvation, *
  my stronghold, so that I shall not be greatly shaken.

3 How long will you assail me to crush me,
all of you together, *
  as if you were a leaning fence, a toppling wall?

4 They seek only to bring me down from my place of honor; *
  lies are their chief delight.

5 They bless with their lips, *
  but in their hearts they curse.

6 For God alone my soul in silence waits; *
  truly, my hope is in God.

7 God alone is my rock and my salvation, *
  my stronghold, so that I shall not be shaken.

8 In God is my safety and my honor; *
    God is my strong rock and my refuge.

9 Put your trust in God always, O people, *
    pour out your hearts before God, who is our refuge.

10 Those of high degree are but a fleeting breath, *
    even those of low estate cannot be trusted.

11 On the scales they are lighter than a breath, *
    all of them together.

12 Put no trust in extortion;
    in robbery take no empty pride; *
        though wealth increase, set not your heart upon it.

13 God has spoken once, twice have I heard it, *
    that power belongs to God.

14 Steadfast love is yours, O Lord, *
    for you repay all people according to their deeds.

63

1 O God, you are my God; eagerly I seek you; *
    my soul thirsts for you, my flesh faints for you,
    as in a barren and dry land where there is no water.

2 Therefore I have gazed upon you in your holy place, *
    that I might behold your power and your glory.

3 For your loving-kindness is better than life itself; *
    my lips shall give you praise.

4 So will I bless you as long as I live *
    and lift up my hands in your name.

5 My soul is content, as with marrow and fatness, *
    and my mouth praises you with joyful lips,

6 When I remember you upon my bed, *
    and meditate on you in the night watches.

7 For you have been my helper, *
    and under the shadow of your wings I will rejoice.

8 My soul clings to you; *
   your right hand holds me fast.

9 May those who seek my life to destroy it *
   go down into the depths of the earth;

10 Let them fall upon the edge of the sword, *
   and let them be food for jackals.

11 But I will rejoice in God;
   all those who swear by God will be glad; *
   for the mouth of those who speak lies shall be stopped.

64

1 Hear my voice, O God, when I complain; *
   protect my life from fear of the enemy.

2 Hide me from the conspiracy of the wicked, *
   from the mob of evildoers.

3 They sharpen their tongue like a sword, *
   and aim their bitter words like arrows,

4 That they may shoot down the blameless from ambush; *
   they shoot without warning and are not afraid.

5 They hold fast to their evil course; *
   they plan how they may hide their snares.

6 They say, "Who will see us?
   who will find out our crimes? *
   we have thought out a perfect plot."

7 The human mind and heart are a mystery; *
   but God will loose an arrow at them,
   and suddenly they will be wounded.

8 God will make them trip over their tongues, *
   and all who see them will shake their heads.

9 Everyone will stand in awe and declare God's deeds; *
   they will recognize God's works.

10 The righteous will rejoice and put their trust in the LORD, *
   and all who are true of heart will glory.

65

1 You are to be praised, O God, in Zion; *
   to you shall vows be performed in Jerusalem.

2 To you that hear prayer shall all flesh come, *
   because of their transgressions.

3 Our sins are stronger than we are, *
   but you will blot them out.

4 Happy are they whom you choose
  and draw to your courts to dwell there! *
   they will be satisfied by the beauty of your house,
   by the holiness of your temple.

5 Awesome things will you show us in your righteousness,
  O God of our salvation, *
   O Hope of all the ends of the earth
   and of the seas that are far away.

6 You make fast the mountains by your power; *
   they are girded about with might.

7 You still the roaring of the seas, *
   the roaring of their waves,
   and the clamor of the peoples.

8 Those who dwell at the ends of the earth will tremble at your
     marvelous signs; *
   you make the dawn and the dusk to sing for joy.

9 You visit the earth and water it abundantly;
  you make it very plenteous; *
   the river of God is full of water.

10 You prepare the grain, *
   for so you provide for the earth.

11 You drench the furrows and smooth out the ridges; *
   with heavy rain you soften the ground and bless its increase.

12 You crown the year with your goodness, *
   and your paths overflow with plenty.

13 May the fields of the wilderness be rich for grazing, *
     and the hills be clothed with joy.

14 May the meadows cover themselves with flocks,
     and the valleys cloak themselves with grain; *
     let them shout for joy and sing.

66

1 Be joyful in God, all you lands; *
     sing the glory of God's name;
     sing the glory of God's praise.

2 Say to God, "How awesome are your deeds! *
     because of your great strength your enemies cringe before you.

3 All the earth bows down before you, *
     sings to you, sings out your name."

4 Come now and see the works of God, *
     how wonderful God's actions toward all people.

5 God turned the sea into dry land,
     so that they went through the water on foot, *
     and there we rejoiced in God.

6 In might God rules for ever
     and keeps watch over the nations; *
     let no rebel rise up against God.

7 Bless our God, you peoples; *
     make the voice of praise to be heard.

8 God holds our souls in life, *
     and will not allow our feet to slip.

9 For you, O God, have proved us; *
     you have tried us just as silver is tried.

10 You brought us into the snare; *
     you laid heavy burdens upon our backs.

11 You let enemies ride over our heads;
     we went through fire and water; *
     but you brought us out into a place of refreshment.

12　I will enter your house with burnt-offerings
　　and will pay you my vows, *
　　　　which I promised with my lips
　　　　and spoke with my mouth when I was in trouble.

13　I will offer you sacrifices of fat beasts
　　with the smoke of rams; *
　　　　I will give you oxen and goats.

14　Come and listen, all you who fear God, *
　　　　and I will tell you what God has done for me.

15　I cried out with my mouth, *
　　　　and God's praise was on my tongue.

16　If I had found evil in my heart, *
　　　　the Lord would not have heard me;

17　But in truth God has heard me *
　　　　and attended to the voice of my prayer.

18　Blessed be God, who has not rejected my prayer, *
　　　　nor withheld steadfast love from me.

67

1　O God, be merciful to us and bless us; *
　　　　show us the light of your countenance and come to us.

2　Let your ways be known upon earth, *
　　　　your saving health among all nations.

3　Let the peoples praise you, O God; *
　　　　let all the peoples praise you.

4　Let the nations be glad and sing for joy, *
　　　　for you judge the peoples with equity
　　　　and guide all the nations upon earth.

5　Let the peoples praise you, O God; *
　　　　let all the peoples praise you.

6　The earth has brought forth its increase; *
　　　　may God, our own God, bless us.

7   O God, give us your blessing; *
      may all the ends of the earth stand in awe of you.

68

1   O God, arise, and let your enemies be scattered; *
      let those who hate you flee before you.

2   Let them vanish like smoke when the wind drives it away; *
      as the wax melts at the fire, so let the wicked perish at the
        presence of God.

3   But let the righteous be glad and rejoice before God; *
      let them also be merry and joyful.

4   Sing to God, sing praises to God's name;
      exalt the One who rides upon the heavens; *
        the name of our God is the LORD; rejoice before the LORD!

5   Defender of widows, father of orphans, *
      God in heaven's holy habitation!

6   God gives the solitary a home and brings forth prisoners into
        freedom; *
      but the rebels shall live in dry places.

7   O God, when you went forth before your people, *
      when you marched through the wilderness,

8   The earth shook, and the skies poured down rain,
      at the presence of God, the God of Sinai, *
        at the presence of God, the God of Israel.

9   You sent a gracious rain, O God, upon your inheritance; *
      you refreshed the land when it was weary.

10 Your people found their home in it; *
      in your goodness, O God, you have made provision for the poor.

11 The Lord gave the word; *
      great was the company of women who bore the tidings:

12 "Kings with their armies are fleeing away; *
      the women at home are dividing the spoils."

13 Though you lingered among the sheepfolds, *
    you shall be like a dove whose wings are covered with silver,
    whose feathers are like green gold.

14 When the Almighty scattered kings, *
    it was like snow falling in Zalmon.

15 O mighty mountain, O hill of Bashan! *
    O rugged mountain, O hill of Bashan!

16 Why do you look with envy, O rugged mountain,
    at the hill on which God chose to rest? *
    truly, the LORD will dwell there for ever.

17 The chariots of God are twenty thousand,
    even thousands of thousands; *
    the Lord comes in holiness from Sinai.

18 You have gone up on high and led captivity captive;
    you have received gifts even from your enemies, *
    that the LORD God might dwell among them.

19 Blessed be the Lord day by day, *
    the God of our salvation, who bears our burdens.

20 You are our God, the God of our salvation; *
    God is the LORD, by whom we escape death.

21 You, O God, shall crush the heads of your enemies, *
    and the hairy scalp of those who go on still in their wickedness.

22 The Lord has said, ''I will bring them back from Bashan; *
    I will bring them back from the depths of the sea;

23 That your foot may be dipped in blood, *
    the tongues of your dogs in the blood of your enemies.''

24 They see your procession, O God, *
    your procession into the sanctuary, my Sovereign and my God.

25 The singers go before, musicians follow after, *
    in the midst of young women playing upon the hand-drums.

26 Bless God in the congregation; *
    bless the LORD, you that are of the fountain of Israel.

27 There is Benjamin, least of the tribes, at the head;
   the princes of Judah in a company; *
      and the princes of Zebulon and Naphtali.

28 Send forth your strength, O God; *
      establish, O God, what you have wrought for us.

29 Rulers shall bring gifts to you, *
      for your temple's sake at Jerusalem.

30 Rebuke the wild beast of the reeds, *
      and the peoples, a herd of wild bulls with its calves.

31 Trample down those who lust after silver; *
      scatter the peoples that delight in war.

32 Let tribute be brought out of Egypt; *
      let Ethiopia stretch out its hands to God.

33 Sing to God, O realms of the earth; *
      sing praises to the Lord.

34 God rides in the heavens, the ancient heavens; *
      God's voice thunders forth, a mighty voice.

35 Ascribe power to God, *
      whose majesty is over Israel,
      whose strength is in the skies.

36 How wonderful is God in the holy places! *
      the God of Israel giving strength and power to the chosen
         people!
      Blessed be God!

69

1 Save me, O God, *
      for the waters have risen up to my neck.

2 I am sinking in deep mire, *
      and there is no firm ground for my feet.

3 I have come into deep waters, *
      and the torrent washes over me.

4 I have grown weary with my crying;
   my throat is inflamed; *
      my eyes have failed from looking for my God.

5 Those who hate me without a cause are more than the hairs of
         my head;
   my lying foes who would destroy me are mighty. *
      Must I then give back what I never stole?

6 O God, you know my foolishness, *
   and my faults are not hidden from you.

7 Let not those who hope in you be put to shame through me,
         Lord GOD of hosts; *
      let not those who seek you be disgraced because of me,
         O God of Israel.

8 Surely, for your sake have I suffered reproach, *
   and shame has covered my face.

9 I have become a stranger to my own kindred, *
   an alien to my mother's children.

10 Zeal for your house has eaten me up; *
    the scorn of those who scorn you has fallen upon me.

11 I humbled myself with fasting, *
    but that was turned to my reproach.

12 I put on sack-cloth also, *
    and became a byword among them.

13 Those who sit at the gate murmur against me, *
    and the drunkards make songs about me.

14 But as for me, this is my prayer to you, *
    at the time you have set, O LORD:

15 "In your great mercy, O God, *
    answer me with your unfailing help.

16 Save me from the mire; do not let me sink; *
    let me be rescued from those who hate me
    and out of the deep waters.

17 Let not the torrent of waters wash over me,
neither let the deep swallow me up; *
    do not let the pit shut its mouth upon me.

18 Answer me, O LORD, for your love is kind; *
    in your great compassion, turn to me.

19 Hide not your face from your servant; *
    be swift and answer me, for I am in distress.

20 Draw near to me and redeem me; *
    because of my enemies deliver me.

21 You know my reproach, my shame, and my dishonor; *
    my adversaries are all in your sight."

22 Reproach has broken my heart, and it cannot be healed; *
    I looked for sympathy, but there was none,
    for comforters, but I could find no one.

23 They gave me gall to eat, *
    and when I was thirsty, they gave me vinegar to drink.

24 Let the table before them be a trap *
    and their sacred feasts a snare.

25 Let their eyes be darkened, that they may not see, *
    and give them continual trembling in their inner parts.

26 Pour out your indignation upon them, *
    and let the fierceness of your anger overtake them.

27 Let their camp be desolate, *
    and let there be none to dwell in their tents.

28 For they persecute the one whom you have stricken *
    and add to the pain of those whom you have pierced.

29 Lay to their charge guilt upon guilt, *
    and let them not receive your vindication.

30 Let them be wiped out of the book of the living *
    and not be written among the righteous.

31 As for me, I am afflicted and in pain; *
    your help, O God, will lift me up on high.

32 I will praise the name of God in song; *
    I will proclaim the greatness of the Lord with thanksgiving.

33 This will please the Lord more than an offering of oxen, *
    more than bullocks with horns and hoofs.

34 The afflicted shall see and be glad; *
    you who seek God, your heart shall live.

35 For the Lord listens to the needy *
    and does not despise those who are in prison.

36 Let the heavens and the earth give praise, *
    the seas and all that moves in them;

37 For God will save Zion and rebuild the cities of Judah; *
    they shall live there and have it in possession.

38 The servants of the Lord will inherit it, *
    and those who love the name of God will dwell therein.

70

1 Be pleased, O God, to deliver me; *
   O Lord, make haste to help me.

2 Let those who seek my life be ashamed
   and altogether dismayed; *
     let those who take pleasure in my misfortune
     draw back and be disgraced.

3 Let those who say to me "Aha!" and gloat over me turn back, *
   because they are ashamed.

4 Let all who seek you rejoice and be glad in you; *
     let those who love your salvation say for ever,
     "Great is the Lord!"

5 But as for me, I am poor and needy; *
   come to me speedily, O God.

6 You are my helper and my deliverer; *
   O Lord, do not tarry.

71

1 In you, O LORD, have I taken refuge; *
  let me never be ashamed.

2 In your righteousness, deliver me and set me free; *
  incline your ear to me and save me.

3 Be my strong rock, a castle to keep me safe; *
  you are my crag and my stronghold.

4 Deliver me, my God, from the hand of the wicked, *
  from the clutches of the evildoer and the oppressor.

5 For you are my hope, O Lord GOD, *
  my confidence since I was young.

6 I have been sustained by you ever since I was born;
  from my mother's womb you have been my strength; *
  my praise shall be always of you.

7 I have become a portent to many; *
  but you are my refuge and my strength.

8 Let my mouth be full of your praise *
  and your glory all the day long.

9 Do not cast me off in my old age; *
  forsake me not when my strength fails.

10 For my enemies are talking against me, *
  and those who lie in wait for my life take counsel together.

11 They say that God has forsaken me,
  that they will come after me and seize me; *
  because there is none who will save.

12 O God, be not far from me; *
  come quickly to help me, O my God.

13 Let those who set themselves against me be put to shame and
    be disgraced; *
  let those who seek to do me evil be covered with scorn and
    reproach.

14 But I shall always wait in patience, *
    and shall praise you more and more.

15 My mouth shall recount your mighty acts
and saving deeds all day long; *
    though I cannot know the number of them.

16 I will begin with the mighty works of the Lord GOD; *
    I will recall your righteousness, yours alone.

17 O God, you have taught me since I was young, *
    and to this day I tell of your wonderful works.

18 And now that I am old and gray-headed, O God, do not
    forsake me, *
    till I make known your strength to this generation
    and your power to all who are to come.

19 Your righteousness, O God, reaches to the heavens; *
    you have done great things;
    who is like you, O God?

20 You have showed me great troubles and adversities, *
    but you will restore my life
    and bring me up again from the deep places of the earth.

21 You strengthen me more and more; *
    you enfold and comfort me.

22 Therefore I will praise you upon the lyre for your faithfulness,
    O my God; *
    I will sing to you with the harp, O Holy One of Israel.

23 My lips will sing with joy when I play to you, *
    and so will my soul, which you have redeemed.

24 My tongue will proclaim your righteousness all day long, *
    for they are ashamed and disgraced who sought to do me harm.

72

1 Give the king your justice, O God, *
    and your righteousness to the king's son;

2 That he may rule your people righteously *
   and the poor with justice;

3 That the mountains may bring prosperity to the people, *
   and the little hills bring righteousness.

4 He shall defend the needy among the people *
   and shall rescue the poor and crush the oppressor.

5 He shall live as long as the sun and moon endure, *
   from one generation to another.

6 He shall come down like rain upon the mown field, *
   like showers that water the earth.

7 In his time shall the righteous flourish; *
   there shall be abundance of peace till the moon shall be no more.

8 He shall rule from sea to sea, *
   and from the river to the ends of the earth.

9 His foes shall bow down before him, *
   and his enemies lick the dust.

10 The kings of Tarshish and of the isles shall pay tribute, *
   and the rulers of Arabia and Saba offer gifts.

11 All kings shall bow down before him, *
   and all the nations do him service.

12 For he shall deliver the poor who cries out in distress, *
   and the oppressed who has no helper.

13 He shall have pity on the lowly and poor *
   and shall preserve the lives of the needy.

14 He shall redeem their lives from oppression and violence, *
   and dear shall their blood be in his sight.

15 Long may he live!
   and may there be given to him gold from Arabia; *
   may prayer be made for him always,
   and may they bless him all the day long.

16 May there be abundance of grain on the earth,
growing thick even on the hilltops; *
    may its fruit flourish like Lebanon,
    and its grain like grass upon the earth.

17 May his name remain for ever
and be established as long as the sun endures; *
    may all the nations bless themselves in him and
    call him blessed.

18 Blessed be the Lord GOD, the God of Israel, *
    who alone does wondrous deeds!

19 And blessed be God's glorious name for ever! *
    and may all the earth be filled with the glory of the LORD.
    Amen. Amen.

73

1 Truly, God is good to Israel, *
    to those who are pure in heart.

2 But as for me, my feet had nearly slipped; *
    I had almost tripped and fallen;

3 Because I envied the proud *
    and saw the prosperity of the wicked:

4 For they suffer no pain, *
    and their bodies are sleek and sound;

5 In the misfortunes of others they have no share; *
    they are not afflicted as others are;

6 Therefore they wear their pride like a necklace *
    and wrap their violence about them like a cloak.

7 Their iniquity comes from gross minds, *
    and their hearts overflow with wicked thoughts.

8 They scoff and speak maliciously; *
    out of their haughtiness they plan oppression.

9 They set their mouths against the heavens, *
    and their evil speech runs through the world.

10 And so the people turn to them *
and find in them no fault.

11 They say, "How should God know? *
is there knowledge in the Most High?"

12 So then, these are the wicked; *
always at ease, they increase their wealth.

13 In vain have I kept my heart clean, *
and washed my hands in innocence.

14 I have been afflicted all day long, *
and punished every morning.

15 Had I gone on speaking this way, *
I should have betrayed the generation of your children.

16 When I tried to understand these things, *
it was too hard for me;

17 Until I entered the sanctuary of God *
and discerned the end of the wicked.

18 Surely, you set them in slippery places; *
you cast them down in ruin.

19 Oh, how suddenly do they come to destruction, *
come to an end, and perish from terror!

20 Like a dream when one awakens, O Lord, *
when you arise you will make their image vanish.

21 When my mind became embittered, *
I was sorely wounded in my heart.

22 I was stupid and had no understanding; *
I was like a brute beast in your presence.

23 Yet I am always with you; *
you hold me by my right hand.

24 You will guide me by your counsel, *
and afterwards receive me with glory.

25 Whom have I in heaven but you? *
   and having you I desire nothing upon earth.

26 Though my flesh and my heart should waste away, *
   God is the strength of my heart and my portion for ever.

27 Truly, those who forsake you will perish; *
   you destroy all who are unfaithful.

28 But it is good for me to be near God; *
   I have made the Lord GOD my refuge.

29 I will speak of all your works *
   in the gates of the city of Zion.

74

1 O God, why have you utterly cast us off? *
  why is your wrath so hot against the sheep of your pasture?

2 Remember your congregation that you purchased long ago, *
  the tribe you redeemed to be your inheritance,
  and Mount Zion where you dwell.

3 Turn your steps toward the endless ruins; *
  the enemy has laid waste everything in your sanctuary.

4 Your adversaries roared in your holy place; *
  they set up their banners as tokens of victory.

5 Like those who come with axes to a grove of trees, *
  they broke down all your carved work with hatchets and
      hammers.

6 They set fire to your holy place; *
  they defiled the dwelling-place of your name
  and razed it to the ground.

7 They said to themselves, "Let us destroy them altogether." *
  They burned down all the meeting-places of God in the land.

8 There are no signs for us to see;
  there is no prophet left; *
  there is not one among us who knows how long.

9 How long, O God, will the adversary scoff? *
   will the enemy blaspheme your name for ever?

10 Why do you draw back your hand? *
   why is your right hand hidden in your bosom?

11 Yet God is my Sovereign from ancient times, *
   victorious in the midst of the earth.

12 You divided the sea by your might *
   and shattered the heads of the dragons upon the waters;

13 You crushed the heads of Leviathan *
   and gave it to the people of the desert for food.

14 You split open spring and torrent; *
   you dried up ever-flowing rivers.

15 Yours is the day, yours also the night; *
   you established the moon and the sun.

16 You fixed all the boundaries of the earth; *
   you made both summer and winter.

17 Remember, O LORD, how the enemy scoffed, *
   how a foolish people despised your name.

18 Do not hand over the life of your dove to wild beasts; *
   never forget the lives of your poor.

19 Look upon your covenant; *
   the dark places of the earth are haunts of violence.

20 Let not the oppressed turn away ashamed; *
   let the poor and needy praise your name.

21 Arise, O God, maintain your cause; *
   remember how fools revile you all day long.

22 Forget not the clamor of your adversaries, *
   the unending tumult of those who rise up against you.

75

1 We give you thanks, O God, we give you thanks, *
   calling upon your name and declaring all your wonderful deeds.

2 "I will appoint a time," says God; *
   "I will judge with equity.

3 Though the earth and all its inhabitants are quaking, *
   I will make its pillars fast.

4 I will say to the boasters, 'Boast no more,' *
   and to the wicked, 'Do not toss your horns;

5 Do not toss your horns so high, *
   nor speak with a proud neck.' "

6 For judgment is neither from the east nor from the west, *
   nor yet from the wilderness or the mountains.

7 It is God who judges, *
   who puts down one and lifts up another.

8 For in the LORD's hand there is a cup,
   full of spiced and foaming wine; *
      the LORD pours it out,
      and all the wicked of the earth shall drink and drain the dregs.

9 But I will rejoice for ever; *
   I will sing praises to the God of Jacob.

10 God shall break off all the horns of the wicked; *
   but the horns of the righteous shall be exalted.

76

1 In Judah is God known; *
   the name of the LORD is great in Israel.

2 At Salem, O God, is your tabernacle, *
   and your dwelling is in Zion.

3 There you broke the flashing arrows, *
   the shield, the sword, and the weapons of battle.

4 How glorious you are! *
   more splendid than the everlasting mountains!

5 The strong of heart have been despoiled;
 they sink into sleep; *
   none of the warriors can lift a hand.

6 At your rebuke, O God of Jacob, *
   both horse and rider lie stunned.

7 What terror you inspire! *
   who can stand before you when you are angry?

8 From heaven you pronounced judgment; *
   the earth was afraid and was still;

9 When God rose up to judgment *
   and to save all the oppressed of the earth.

10 Truly, wrathful Edom will give you thanks, *
   and the remnant of Hamath will keep your feasts.

11 Make a vow to the LORD your God and keep it; *
   let all around God bring gifts to the One who is worthy to
     be feared.

12 The LORD breaks the spirit of rulers, *
   and strikes terror in the kings of the earth.

77

1 I will cry aloud to God; *
   I will cry aloud, and God will hear me.

2 In the day of my trouble I sought the Lord; *
   my hands were stretched out by night and did not tire;
   I refused to be comforted.

3 I think of God, I am restless, *
   I ponder, and my spirit faints.

4 You will not let my eyelids close; *
   I am troubled and I cannot speak.

5 I consider the days of old; *
   I remember the years long past;

6 I commune with my heart in the night; *
   I ponder and search my mind.

7 Will the Lord cast me off for ever *
   and show favor to me no more?

8 Has the loving-kindness of the LORD come to an end? *
   has God's promise failed for evermore?

9 Has God forgotten to be gracious, *
   and in anger withheld compassion?

10 And I said, "My grief is this: *
   the right hand of the Most High has lost its power."

11 I will remember the works of the LORD, *
   and call to mind your wonders of old time.

12 I will meditate on all your acts *
   and ponder your mighty deeds.

13 Your way, O God, is holy; *
   who is so great a god as our God?

14 You are the God who works wonders *
   and have declared your power among the peoples.

15 By your strength you have redeemed your people, *
   the children of Jacob and Joseph.

16 The waters saw you, O God;
   the waters saw you and trembled; *
   the very depths were shaken.

17 The clouds poured out water;
   the skies thundered; *
   your arrows flashed to and fro;

18 The sound of your thunder was in the whirlwind;
   your lightnings lit up the world; *
   the earth trembled and shook.

19 Your way was in the sea,
   and your paths in the great waters, *
   yet your footsteps were not seen.

20 You led your people like a flock *
  by the hand of Moses and Aaron.

78

1 Hear my teaching, O my people; *
  incline your ears to the words of my mouth.

2 I will open my mouth in a parable; *
  I will declare the mysteries of ancient times.

3 That which we have heard and known,
 and what our ancestors have told us, *
  we will not hide from their children.

4 We will recount to generations to come
 the praiseworthy deeds and the power of the LORD, *
  and the wonderful works God has done.

5 God set up decrees for Jacob
 and established a law for Israel, *
  commanding them to teach it to their children;

6 That the generations to come might know,
 and the children yet unborn; *
  that they in their turn might tell it to their children;

7 So that they might put their trust in God, *
  and not forget the deeds of God,
  but keep God's commandments;

8 And not be like their ancestors,
 a stubborn and rebellious generation, *
  a generation whose heart was not steadfast,
  and whose spirit was not faithful to God.

9 The people of Ephraim, armed with the bow, *
  turned back in the day of battle;

10 They did not keep the covenant of God, *
  and refused to walk in God's law;

11 They forgot what God had done, *
  and the wonders shown to them.

12 God worked marvels in the sight of their ancestors, *
    in the land of Egypt, in the field of Zoan.

13 God split open the sea and let them pass through, *
    making the waters stand up like walls.

14 God led them with a cloud by day, *
    and all the night through with a glow of fire.

15 God split the hard rocks in the wilderness *
    and gave them drink as from the great deep.

16 God brought streams out of the cliff, *
    and the waters gushed out like rivers.

17 But they went on sinning against the LORD, *
    rebelling in the desert against the Most High.

18 They tested God in their hearts, *
    demanding food for their craving.

19 They railed against God and said, *
    "Can God set a table in the wilderness?

20 True, God struck the rock, the waters gushed out, and the
    gullies overflowed; *
    but is God able to give bread
    or to provide meat for this people?"

21 Hearing this, the LORD was full of wrath; *
    a fire was kindled against Jacob,
    the LORD's anger mounted against Israel;

22 For they had no faith in God, *
    nor did they put their trust in the LORD's saving power.

23 So God commanded the clouds above *
    and opened the doors of heaven.

24 God rained down manna upon them to eat *
    and gave them grain from heaven.

25 So mortals ate the bread of angels; *
    God provided for them food enough.

26 God caused the east wind to blow in the heavens *
  and mightily led out the south wind.

27 God rained down flesh upon them like dust *
  and winged birds like the sand of the sea.

28 God let it fall in the midst of their camp *
  and round about their dwellings.

29 So they ate and were well filled, *
  for the LORD gave them what they craved.

30 But they did not stop their craving, *
  though the food was still in their mouths.

31 So God's anger mounted against them; *
  God slew all their strongest
  and laid low the youth of Israel.

32 In spite of all this, they went on sinning *
  and had no faith in God's wonderful works.

33 So God brought their days to an end like a breath *
  and their years in sudden terror.

34 Whenever God slew them, they would repent, *
  and they would diligently search for God.

35 They would remember that God was their rock, *
  and the Most High God their redeemer.

36 But they flattered God with their mouths *
  and lied to God with their tongues.

37 Their heart was not steadfast toward God, *
  and they were not faithful to the covenant.

38 But being so merciful, God forgave their sins
  and did not destroy them; *
  many times God held back anger
  and did not permit divine wrath to be roused.

39 For the LORD remembered that they were but flesh, *
  a breath that goes forth and does not return.

40 How often the people disobeyed God in the wilderness *
and offended the LORD in the desert!

41 Again and again they tempted God *
and provoked the Holy One of Israel.

42 They did not remember God's power *
in the day when God ransomed them from the enemy;

43 How God wrought signs in Egypt *
and omens in the field of Zoan.

44 God turned their rivers into blood, *
so that they could not drink of their streams.

45 God sent swarms of flies among them, which ate them up, *
and frogs, which destroyed them.

46 God gave their crops to the caterpillar, *
the fruit of their toil to the locust.

47 God killed their vines with hail *
and their sycamores with frost.

48 God delivered their cattle to hailstones *
and their livestock to hot thunderbolts.

49 God poured out upon them blazing anger: *
fury, indignation, and distress,
a troop of destroying angels.

50 God gave full rein to divine anger;
God did not spare their souls from death; *
but delivered their lives to the plague.

51 God struck down all the firstborn of Egypt, *
the flower of manhood in the dwellings of Ham.

52 God led out the chosen people like sheep *
and guided them in the wilderness like a flock.

53 God led them to safety, and they were not afraid; *
but the sea overwhelmed their enemies.

54 God brought them to the holy land, *
to the mountain won by God's own hand.

55 The LORD drove out the Canaanites before them
    and apportioned an inheritance to them by lot; *
        God made the tribes of Israel to dwell in their tents.

56 But they tested and defied the LORD, *
        and did not keep the commandments of the Most High.

57 They turned away and were disloyal like their ancestors; *
        they were undependable like a warped bow.

58 They grieved God with their hill-altars *
        and provoked God's displeasure with their idols.

59 Hearing this, God was angry *
        and utterly rejected Israel.

60 God forsook the shrine at Shiloh, *
        the tabernacle where God had lived among mortals.

61 God delivered the ark into captivity, *
        God's glory into the adversary's hand.

62 God gave the chosen people to the sword *
        and was mightily angered against them.

63 The fire consumed their young men; *
        there were no wedding songs for their young women.

64 Their priests fell by the sword, *
        and their widows made no lamentation.

65 Then the LORD woke as though from sleep, *
        like a warrior refreshed with wine.

66 These enemies God struck on the backside *
        and put them to perpetual shame.

67 God rejected the tent of Joseph *
        and did not choose the tribe of Ephraim;

68 God chose instead the tribe of Judah *
        and Mount Zion, the beloved.

69 God built the holy sanctuary like the heights of heaven, *
        like the earth which God founded for ever.

70 God chose David to serve, *
  and took him away from the sheepfolds.

71 God brought him from tending the sheep, *
  to be a shepherd over Jacob, the chosen people,
  and over Israel, the chosen inheritance.

72 So David shepherded them with a faithful and true heart *
  and guided them with the skillfulness of his hands.

79

1 O God, the heathen have come into your inheritance;
  they have profaned your holy temple; *
    they have made Jerusalem a heap of rubble.

2 They have given the bodies of your servants as food for the
      birds of the air, *
  and the flesh of your faithful ones to the beasts of the field.

3 They have shed their blood like water on every side of Jerusalem, *
  and there was no one to bury them.

4 We have become a reproach to our neighbors, *
  an object of scorn and derision to those around us.

5 How long will you be angry, O LORD? *
  will your fury blaze like fire for ever?

6 Pour out your wrath upon the heathen who have not known
      you *
  and upon the realms that have not called upon your name.

7 For they have devoured the people of Jacob *
  and made their dwelling a ruin.

8 Remember not our past sins;
  let your compassion be swift to meet us; *
    for we have been brought very low.

9 Help us, O God our Savior, for the glory of your name; *
  deliver us and forgive us our sins, for your name's sake.

10 Why should the heathen say, "Where is their God?" *
  Let it be known among the heathen and in our sight
  that you avenge the shedding of your servants' blood.

11 Let the sorrowful sighing of the prisoners come before you, *
  and by your great might spare those who are condemned to die.

12 May the revilings with which they reviled you, O Lord, *
  return seven-fold into their bosoms.

13 For we are your people and the sheep of your pasture; *
  we will give you thanks for ever
  and show forth your praise from age to age.

80

1 Hear, O Shepherd of Israel, leading Joseph like a flock; *
  shine forth, you that are enthroned upon the cherubim.

2 In the presence of Ephraim, Benjamin, and Manasseh, *
  stir up your strength and come to help us.

3 Restore us, O God of hosts; *
  show the light of your countenance, and we shall be saved.

4 O LORD God of hosts, *
  how long will you be angered
  despite the prayers of your people?

5 You have fed them with the bread of tears; *
  you have given them bowls of tears to drink.

6 You have made us the derision of our neighbors, *
  and our enemies laugh us to scorn.

7 Restore us, O God of hosts; *
  show the light of your countenance, and we shall be saved.

8 You have brought a vine out of Egypt; *
  you cast out the nations and planted it.

9 You prepared the ground for it; *
  it took root and filled the land.

10 The mountains were covered by its shadow *
    and the towering cedar trees by its boughs.

11 You stretched out its tendrils to the sea *
    and its branches to the river.

12 Why have you broken down its wall, *
    so that all who pass by pluck off its grapes?

13 The wild boar of the forest has ravaged it, *
    and the beasts of the field have grazed upon it.

14 Turn now, O God of hosts, look down from heaven;
    behold and tend this vine; *
    preserve what your right hand has planted.

15 They burn it with fire like rubbish; *
    at the rebuke of your countenance let them perish.

16 Let your hand be upon the one at your right hand, *
    the one you have made so strong for yourself.

17 And so will we never turn away from you; *
    give us life, that we may call upon your name.

18 Restore us, O LORD God of hosts; *
    show the light of your countenance, and we shall be saved.

81

1 Sing with joy to God our strength *
   and raise a loud shout to the God of Jacob.

2 Raise a song and sound the timbrel, *
   the merry harp, and the lyre.

3 Blow the ram's-horn at the new moon, *
   and at the full moon, the day of our feast.

4 For this is a statute for Israel, *
   a law of the God of Jacob.

5 God laid it as a solemn charge upon Joseph, *
   when the people came out of the land of Egypt.

6 I heard an unfamiliar voice saying, *
    "I eased their shoulder from the burden;
      their hands were set free from bearing the load.

7 You called on me in trouble, and I saved you; *
    I answered you from the secret place of thunder
    and tested you at the waters of Meribah.

8 Hear, O my people, and I will admonish you: *
    O Israel, if you would but listen to me!

9 There shall be no strange god among you; *
    you shall not worship a foreign god.

10 I am the Lord your God,
    who brought you out of the land of Egypt and said, *
      'Open your mouth wide, and I will fill it.'

11 And yet my people did not hear my voice, *
    and Israel would not obey me.

12 So I gave them over to the stubbornness of their hearts, *
    to follow their own devices.

13 Oh, that my people would listen to me! *
    that Israel would walk in my ways!

14 I should soon subdue their enemies *
    and turn my hand against their foes.

15 Those who hate the Lord would cringe before me, *
    and their punishment would last for ever.

16 But Israel would I feed with the finest wheat *
    and satisfy them with honey from the rock."

82

1 God arises in the council of heaven *
    and gives judgment in the midst of the gods:

2 "How long will you judge unjustly, *
    and show favor to the wicked?

3 Save the weak and the orphan; *
   defend the humble and needy;

4 Rescue the weak and the poor; *
   deliver them from the power of the wicked.

5 They do not know, neither do they understand;
   they go about in darkness; *
   all the foundations of the earth are shaken.

6 Now I say to you, 'You are gods, *
   and all of you children of the Most High;

7 Nevertheless, you shall die like mortals, *
   and fall like any leader.' ''

8 Arise, O God, and rule the earth, *
   for you shall take all nations for your own.

83

1 O God, do not be silent; *
   do not keep still nor hold your peace, O God;

2 For your enemies are in tumult, *
   and those who hate you have lifted up their heads.

3 They take secret counsel against your people *
   and plot against those whom you protect.

4 They have said, "Come, let us wipe them out from among the
      nations; *
   let the name of Israel be remembered no more."

5 They have conspired together; *
   they have made an alliance against you:

6 The tents of Edom and the Ishmaelites; *
   the Moabites and the Hagarenes;

7 Gebal, and Ammon, and Amalek; *
   the Philistines and those who dwell in Tyre.

8 The Assyrians also have joined them, *
   and have come to help the people of Lot.

9　Do to them as you did to Midian, *
　　to Sisera, and to Jabin at the river of Kishon:

10　They were destroyed at Endor; *
　　they became like dung upon the ground.

11　Make their leaders like Oreb and Zeeb, *
　　and all their commanders like Zebah and Zalmunna,

12　Who said, "Let us take for ourselves *
　　the fields of God as our possession."

13　O my God, make them like whirling dust *
　　and like chaff before the wind;

14　Like fire that burns down a forest, *
　　like the flame that sets mountains ablaze.

15　Drive them with your tempest *
　　and terrify them with your storm;

16　Cover their faces with shame, O LORD, *
　　that they may seek your name.

17　Let them be disgraced and terrified for ever; *
　　let them be put to confusion and perish.

18　Let them know that you, whose name is the LORD, *
　　you alone are the Most High over all the earth.

84

1　How dear to me is your dwelling, O LORD of hosts! *
　　My soul has a desire and longing for the courts of the LORD;
　　my heart and my flesh rejoice in the living God.

2　The sparrow has found her a house
　　and the swallow a nest where she may lay her young; *
　　by the side of your altars, O LORD of hosts,
　　my Sovereign and my God.

3　Happy are they who dwell in your house! *
　　they will always be praising you.

4   Happy are the people whose strength is in you! *
    whose hearts are set on the pilgrims' way.

5   Those who go through the desolate valley will find it a place
        of springs, *
    for the early rains have covered it with pools of water.

6   They will climb from height to height, *
    and the God of gods will appear in Zion.

7   Lord God of hosts, hear my prayer; *
    hearken, O God of Jacob.

8   Behold our defender, O God; *
    and look upon the face of your anointed.

9   For one day in your courts is better than a thousand in my
        own room, *
    and to stand at the threshold of the house of my God
    than to dwell in the tents of the wicked.

10 For the Lord God is both sun and shield; *
    the Lord will give grace and glory;

11 No good thing will the Lord withhold *
    from those who walk with integrity.

12 O Lord of hosts, *
    happy are they who put their trust in you!

85

1   You have been gracious to your land, O Lord, *
    you have restored the good fortune of Jacob.

2   You have forgiven the iniquity of your people *
    and blotted out all their sins.

3   You have withdrawn all your fury *
    and turned yourself from your wrathful indignation.

4   Restore us then, O God our Savior; *
    let your anger depart from us.

5 Will you be displeased with us for ever? *
　　will you prolong your anger from age to age?

6 Will you not give us life again, *
　　that your people may rejoice in you?

7 Show us your mercy, O LORD, *
　　and grant us your salvation.

8 I will listen, O LORD God, to what you are saying, *
　　for you are speaking peace to your faithful people
　　and to those who turn their hearts to you.

9 Truly, your salvation is very near to those who fear you, *
　　that your glory may dwell in our land.

10 Mercy and truth have met together; *
　　righteousness and peace have kissed each other.

11 Truth shall spring up from the earth, *
　　and righteousness shall look down from heaven.

12 O LORD, you will indeed grant prosperity, *
　　and our land will yield its increase.

13 Righteousness shall go before you, *
　　and peace shall be a pathway for your feet.

86

1 Bow down your ear, O LORD, and answer me, *
　　for I am poor and in misery.

2 Keep watch over my life, for I am faithful; *
　　save your servant, for I put my trust in you.

3 Be merciful to me, O LORD, for you are my God; *
　　I call upon you all the day long.

4 Gladden the soul of your servant, *
　　for to you, O LORD, I lift up my soul.

5 For you, O LORD, are good and forgiving, *
 and great is your love toward all who call upon you.

6 Give ear, O LORD, to my prayer, *
 and attend to the voice of my supplications.

7 In the time of my trouble I will call upon you, *
 for you will answer me.

8 Among the gods there is none like you, O LORD, *
 nor anything like your works.

9 All nations you have made will come and worship you, O LORD, *
 and glorify your name.

10 For you are great;
 you do wondrous things; *
 and you alone are God.

11 Teach me your way, O LORD,
 and I will walk in your truth; *
 knit my heart to you that I may fear your name.

12 I will thank you, O LORD my God, with all my heart, *
 and glorify your name for evermore.

13 For great is your love toward me; *
 you have delivered me from the nethermost pit.

14 The arrogant rise up against me, O God,
 and a violent mob seeks my life; *
 they have not set you before their eyes.

15 But you, O LORD, are gracious and full of compassion, *
 slow to anger, and full of kindness and truth.

16 Turn to me and have mercy upon me; *
 give your strength to your servant;
 and save the child of your handmaid.

17 Show me a sign of your favor,
 so that those who hate me may see it and be ashamed; *
 because you, O LORD, have helped me and comforted me.

87

1 On the holy mountain stands the city God has founded; *
  the LORD loves the gates of Zion
  more than all the dwellings of Jacob.

2 Glorious things are spoken of you, *
  O city of our God.

3 I count Egypt and Babylon among those who know me; *
  behold Philistia, Tyre, and Ethiopia:
  in Zion were they born.

4 Of the city it shall be said, "Everyone was born in Zion, *
  and the Most High shall sustain it."

5 Enrolling the people, the LORD will record, *
  "These also were born there."

6 The singers and the dancers will say, *
  "All my fresh springs are in you."

88

1 O LORD, my God, my Savior, *
  by day and night I cry to you.

2 Let my prayer enter into your presence; *
  incline your ear to my lamentation.

3 For I am full of trouble; *
  my life is at the brink of the grave.

4 I am counted among those who go down to the pit; *
  I have become like one who has no strength;

5 Lost among the dead, *
  like the slain who lie in the grave,

6 Whom you remember no more, *
  for they are cut off from your hand.

7 You have laid me in the depths of the pit, *
  in dark places, and in the abyss.

8 Your anger weighs upon me heavily, *
   and all your great waves overwhelm me.

9 You have put my friends far from me;
   you have made me to be abhorred by them; *
   I am in prison and cannot get free.

10 My sight has failed me because of trouble; *
   LORD, I have called upon you daily;
   I have stretched out my hands to you.

11 Do you work wonders for the dead? *
   will those who have died stand up and give you thanks?

12 Will your loving-kindness be declared in the grave? *
   your faithfulness in the land of destruction?

13 Will your wonders be known in the dark? *
   or your righteousness in the country where all is forgotten?

14 But as for me, O LORD, I cry to you for help; *
   in the morning my prayer comes before you.

15 LORD, why have you rejected me? *
   why have you hidden your face from me?

16 Ever since my youth, I have been wretched and at the point
      of death; *
   I have borne your terrors with a troubled mind.

17 Your blazing anger has swept over me; *
   your terrors have destroyed me;

18 They surround me all day long like a flood; *
   they encompass me on every side.

19 My friend and my neighbor you have put away from me, *
   and darkness is my only companion.

89

1 Your love, O LORD, for ever will I sing; *
   from age to age my mouth will proclaim your faithfulness.

2 For I am persuaded that your love is established for ever; *
   you have set your faithfulness firmly in the heavens.

3 "I have made a covenant with my chosen one; *
   I have sworn an oath to David my servant:

4 'I will establish your line for ever, *
   and preserve your throne for all generations.' "

5 The heavens bear witness to your wonders, O LORD, *
   and to your faithfulness in the assembly of the holy ones;

6 For who in the skies can be compared to the LORD? *
   who is like the LORD among the gods?

7 God is much to be feared in the council of the holy ones, *
   great and terrible to all those circled around.

8 Who is like you, LORD God of hosts? *
   O mighty LORD, your faithfulness is all around you.

9 You rule the raging of the sea *
   and still the surging of its waves.

10 You have crushed Rahab of the deep with a deadly wound; *
   you have scattered your enemies with your mighty arm.

11 Yours are the heavens; the earth also is yours; *
   you laid the foundations of the world and all that is in it.

12 You have made the north and the south; *
   Tabor and Hermon rejoice in your name.

13 You have a mighty arm; *
   strong is your hand and high is your right hand.

14 Righteousness and justice are the foundations of your throne; *
   love and truth go before your face.

15 Happy are the people who know the festal shout! *
   they walk, O LORD, in the light of your presence.

16 They rejoice daily in your name; *
   they are jubilant in your righteousness.

17 For you are the glory of their strength, *
    and by your favor our might is exalted.

18 Truly, the LORD is our ruler; *
    the Holy One of Israel is our Sovereign.

19 You spoke once in a vision and said to your faithful people: *
    ''I have set the crown upon a warrior
    and have exalted one chosen out of the people.

20 I have found David my servant; *
    with my holy oil have I anointed him.

21 My hand will hold him fast *
    and my arm will make him strong.

22 No enemy shall deceive him, *
    nor any wicked man bring him down.

23 I will crush his foes before him *
    and strike down those who hate him.

24 My faithfulness and love shall be with him, *
    and he shall be victorious through my name.

25 I shall make his dominion extend *
    from the great sea to the river.

26 He will say to me, 'You are my father, *
    my God, and the rock of my salvation.'

27 I will make him my firstborn *
    and higher than the rulers of the earth.

28 I will keep my love for him for ever, *
    and my covenant will stand firm for him.

29 I will establish his line for ever *
    and his throne as the days of heaven.

30 If his children forsake my law *
    and do not walk according to my judgments;

31 If they break my statutes *
    and do not keep my commandments;

32 I will punish their transgressions with a rod *
    and their iniquities with the lash;

33 But I will not take my love from him, *
    nor let my faithfulness prove false.

34 I will not break my covenant, *
    nor change what has gone out of my lips.

35 Once for all I have sworn by my holiness: *
    'I will not lie to David.

36 His line shall endure for ever *
    and his throne as the sun before me;

37 It shall stand fast for evermore like the moon, *
    the abiding witness in the sky.' "

38 But you have cast off and rejected your anointed; *
    you have become enraged at him.

39 You have broken your covenant with your servant, *
    defiled his crown, and hurled it to the ground.

40 You have breached all his walls *
    and laid his strongholds in ruins.

41 All who pass by despoil him; *
    he has become the scorn of his neighbors.

42 You have exalted the right hand of his foes *
    and made all his enemies rejoice.

43 You have turned back the edge of his sword *
    and have not sustained him in battle.

44 You have put an end to his splendor *
    and cast his throne to the ground.

45 You have cut short the days of his youth *
    and have covered him with shame.

46 How long will you hide yourself, O LORD?
    will you hide yourself for ever? *
    how long will your anger burn like fire?

47 Remember, LORD, how short life is, *
how frail you have made all flesh.

48 Who can live and not see death? *
who can escape from the power of the grave?

49 Where, Lord, are your loving-kindnesses of old, *
which you promised David in your faithfulness?

50 Remember, Lord, how your servant is mocked, *
how I carry in my bosom the taunts of many peoples,

51 The taunts your enemies have hurled, O LORD, *
which they hurled at the heels of your anointed.

52 Blessed be the LORD for evermore! *
Amen, I say, Amen.

90

1 Lord, you have been our refuge *
from one generation to another.

2 Before the mountains were brought forth,
or the land and the earth were born, *
from age to age you are God.

3 You turn us back to the dust and say, *
"Go back, O child of earth."

4 For a thousand years in your sight are like yesterday when it
is past *
and like a watch in the night.

5 You sweep us away like a dream; *
we fade away suddenly like the grass.

6 In the morning it is green and flourishes; *
in the evening it is dried up and withered.

7 For we consume away in your displeasure; *
we are afraid because of your wrathful indignation.

8 Our iniquities you have set before you, *
and our secret sins in the light of your countenance.

9 When you are angry, all our days are gone; *
     we bring our years to an end like a sigh.

10 The span of our life is seventy years,
     perhaps in strength even eighty; *
         yet the sum of them is but labor and sorrow,
         for they pass away quickly and we are gone.

11 Who regards the power of your wrath? *
     who rightly fears your indignation?

12 So teach us to number our days *
     that we may apply our hearts to wisdom.

13 Return, O LORD; how long will you tarry? *
     be gracious to your servants.

14 Satisfy us by your loving-kindness in the morning; *
     so shall we rejoice and be glad all the days of our life.

15 Make us glad by the measure of the days that you afflicted us *
     and the years in which we suffered adversity.

16 Show your servants your works *
     and your splendor to their children.

17 May the graciousness of the LORD our God be upon us; *
     prosper the work of our hands;
     prosper our handiwork.

91

1 You who dwell in the shelter of the Most High, *
     abide under the shadow of the Almighty.

2 You shall say to the LORD,
     "You are my refuge and my stronghold, *
     my God in whom I put my trust."

3 God shall deliver you from the snare of the hunter *
     and from the deadly pestilence.

4 God's pinions will cover you,
     and you shall find refuge under the wings of the LORD, *
         whose faithfulness shall be a shield and buckler.

124

5 You shall not be afraid of any terror by night, *
   nor of the arrow that flies by day;

6 Of the plague that stalks in the darkness, *
   nor of the sickness that lays waste at mid-day.

7 A thousand shall fall at your side
and ten thousand at your right hand, *
   but it shall not come near you.

8 Your eyes have only to behold *
   to see the reward of the wicked.

9 Because you have made the LORD your refuge, *
   and the Most High your habitation,

10 There shall no evil happen to you, *
   neither shall any plague come near your dwelling.

11 For God shall give the holy angels charge over you, *
   to keep you in all your ways.

12 They shall bear you in their hands, *
   lest you dash your foot against a stone.

13 You shall tread upon the lion and adder; *
   you shall trample the young lion and the serpent under your feet.

14 Because they are bound to me in love,
therefore will I deliver them; *
   I will protect them, because they know my name.

15 They shall call upon me, and I will answer them; *
I am with them in trouble;
   I will rescue them and bring them to honor.

16 With long life will I satisfy them, *
   and show them my salvation.

92

1 It is a good thing to give thanks to the LORD, *
   and to sing praises to your name, O Most High;

2 To tell of your loving-kindness early in the morning *
   and of your faithfulness in the night season;

3 On the psaltery, and on the lyre, *
   and to the melody of the harp.

4 For you have made me glad by your acts, O LORD; *
   and I shout for joy because of the works of your hands.

5 LORD, how great are your works! *
   your thoughts are very deep.

6 The dullard does not know,
   nor does the fool understand, *
      that though the wicked grow like weeds,
      and all the workers of iniquity flourish,

7 They flourish only to be destroyed for ever; *
   but you, O LORD, are exalted for evermore.

8 For lo, your enemies, O LORD,
   lo, your enemies shall perish, *
      and all the workers of iniquity shall be scattered.

9 But my horn you have exalted like the horns of wild bulls; *
   I am anointed with fresh oil.

10 My eyes also gloat over my enemies, *
   and my ears rejoice to hear the doom of the wicked who rise
      up against me.

11 The righteous shall flourish like a palm tree, *
   and shall spread abroad like a cedar of Lebanon.

12 Those who are planted in the house of the LORD *
   shall flourish in the courts of our God;

13 They shall still bear fruit in old age; *
   they shall be green and succulent;

14 That they may show how upright the LORD is, *
   my Rock, in whom there is no fault.

93

1　You, O LORD, are Sovereign;
　　you have put on splendid apparel; *
　　　You, O LORD, have put on your apparel
　　　and girded yourself with strength.

2　You have made the whole world so sure *
　　that it cannot be moved;

3　Ever since the world began, your throne has been established; *
　　you are from everlasting.

4　The waters have lifted up, O LORD,
　　the waters have lifted up their voice; *
　　　the waters have lifted up their pounding waves.

5　Mightier than the sound of many waters,
　　mightier than the breakers of the sea, *
　　　mightier is the LORD who dwells on high.

6　Your testimonies are very sure, *
　　and holiness adorns your house, O LORD,
　　for ever and for evermore.

94

1　O LORD God of vengeance, *
　　O God of vengeance, show yourself.

2　Rise up, O Judge of the world; *
　　give the arrogant their just deserts.

3　How long shall the wicked, O LORD, *
　　how long shall the wicked triumph?

4　They bluster in their insolence; *
　　all evildoers are full of boasting.

5　They crush your people, O LORD, *
　　and afflict your chosen nation.

6　They murder the widow and the stranger *
　　and put the orphans to death.

7 Yet they say, "The LORD does not see, *
the God of Jacob takes no notice."

8 Consider well, you dullards among the people; *
when will you fools understand?

9 Does the One who planted the ear not hear? *
does the One who formed the eye not see?

10 Does the One who admonishes the nations not punish? *
does the One who teaches all the world have no knowledge?

11 The LORD knows our human thoughts; *
how like a puff of wind they are.

12 Happy are they whom you instruct, O LORD! *
whom you teach out of your law;

13 To give them rest in evil days, *
until a pit is dug for the wicked.

14 For you, O LORD, will not abandon your people, *
nor will you forsake your own.

15 For judgment will again be just, *
and all the true of heart will follow it.

16 Who rose up for me against the wicked? *
who took my part against the evildoers?

17 If the LORD had not come to my help, *
I should soon have dwelt in the land of silence.

18 As often as I said, "My foot has slipped," *
your love, O LORD, upheld me.

19 When many cares fill my mind, *
your consolations cheer my soul.

20 Can a corrupt tribunal have any part with you, *
one which frames evil into law?

21 They conspire against the life of the just *
and condemn the innocent to death.

22 But the LORD has become my stronghold, *
   and my God the rock of my trust.

23 The LORD will turn their wickedness back upon them
   and destroy them in their own malice; *
   the LORD our God will destroy them.

95

1 Come, let us sing to the LORD; *
   let us shout for joy to the Rock of our salvation.

2 Let us come before God's presence with thanksgiving *
   and raise a loud shout to the LORD with psalms.

3 For the LORD is a great God, *
   and a great Sovereign above all gods.

4 The LORD holds the caverns of the earth, *
   and sustains the heights of the hills.

5 The sea belongs to God, who made it, *
   whose hands have molded the dry land.

6 Come, let us bow down, and bend the knee, *
   and kneel before the LORD our Maker.

7 For the LORD is our God,
   and we are the people of God's pasture and the sheep of
       God's hand. *
   Oh, that today you would hearken to God's voice!

8 Harden not your hearts,
   as your ancestors did in the wilderness, *
       at Meribah, and on that day at Massah,
   when they tempted me.

9 They put me to the test, *
   though they had seen my works.

10 Forty years long I detested that generation and said, *
   "This people are wayward in their hearts;
   they do not know my ways."

11 So I swore in my wrath, *
    "They shall not enter into my rest."

96

1 Sing to the LORD a new song; *
    sing to the LORD, all the whole earth.

2 Sing to the LORD and bless the LORD's name; *
    proclaim the good news of salvation from day to day.

3 Declare the glory of the LORD among the nations *
    and the wonders of the LORD among all peoples.

4 For great is the LORD and greatly to be praised, *
    more to be feared than all gods.

5 As for all the gods of the nations, they are but idols; *
    but it is the LORD who made the heavens.

6 Oh, the majesty and magnificence of the presence of the LORD! *
    Oh, the power and the splendor of the sanctuary of our God!

7 Ascribe to the LORD, you families of the peoples; *
    ascribe to the LORD honor and power.

8 Ascribe to the LORD the honor due the divine name; *
    come to the holy courts with your offerings.

9 Worship the LORD in the beauty of holiness; *
    let the whole earth tremble in awe.

10 Tell it out among the nations: "The LORD is Sovereign! *
    the LORD has made the world so firm that it cannot be moved
    and will judge the peoples with equity."

11 Let the heavens rejoice, and let the earth be glad;
    let the sea thunder and all that is in it; *
    let the field be joyful and all that is therein.

12 Then shall all the trees of the wood shout for joy
    before the LORD who is coming, *
    who is coming to judge the earth.

13 The LORD will judge the world with righteousness *
    and the peoples with truth.

97

1 The LORD is Sovereign;
   let the earth rejoice; *
     let the multitude of the isles be glad.

2 Clouds and darkness are round about you, *
   righteousness and justice are the foundations of your throne.

3 A fire goes before you *
   and burns up your enemies on every side.

4 Your lightnings light up the world; *
   the earth sees it and is afraid.

5 The mountains melt like wax at the presence of the LORD, *
   at the presence of the Lord of the whole earth.

6 The heavens declare your righteousness, O LORD, *
   and all the peoples see your glory.

7 Confounded be all who worship carved images
   and delight in false gods! *
     Bow down before the LORD, all you gods.

8 Zion hears and is glad, and the cities of Judah rejoice, *
   because of your judgments, O LORD.

9 For you are the LORD,
   most high over all the earth; *
     you are exalted far above all gods.

10 The LORD loves those who hate evil; *
    the LORD preserves the lives of the faithful
    and delivers them from the hand of the wicked.

11 Light has sprung up for the righteous, *
    and joyful gladness for those who are truehearted.

12 Rejoice in the LORD, you righteous, *
    and to the holy name of the LORD give your praise.

98

1 Sing to the LORD a new song, *
   for the LORD has done marvelous things.

2 The right hand and the holy arm of the LORD *
   have secured the victory.

3 The LORD has made known this victory *
   and has openly shown righteousness in the sight of the nations.

4 The LORD remembers mercy and faithfulness to the house of
      Israel, *
   and all the ends of the earth have seen the victory of our God.

5 Shout with joy to the LORD, all you lands; *
   lift up your voice, rejoice, and sing.

6 Sing to the LORD with the harp, *
   with the harp and the voice of song.

7 With trumpets and the sound of the horn *
   shout with joy before the Sovereign, the LORD.

8 Let the sea make a noise and all that is in it, *
   the lands and those who dwell therein.

9 Let the rivers clap their hands, *
   and let the hills ring out with joy before the LORD,
   who is coming to judge the earth.

10 In righteousness shall the LORD judge the world *
   and the peoples with equity.

99

1 The LORD is Sovereign;
   let the people tremble; *
      the LORD is enthroned upon the cherubim;
      let the earth shake.

2 The LORD is great in Zion *
   and is high above all peoples.

3 Let them confess the name of the LORD,
   which is great and awesome; *
      the LORD is the Holy One.

4 "O mighty Sovereign, lover of justice,
   you have established equity; *
      you have executed justice and righteousness in Jacob."

5 Proclaim the greatness of the LORD our God, *
   and fall down before the footstool of the Holy One.

6 Moses and Aaron among your priests,
   and Samuel among those who call upon your name, *
      they called upon you, O LORD, and you answered them.

7 You spoke to them out of the pillar of cloud; *
   they kept your testimonies and the decree that you gave them.

8 O LORD our God, you answered them indeed; *
   you were a God who forgave them,
      yet punished them for their evil deeds.

9 Proclaim the greatness of the LORD our God
   and worship upon God's holy hill; *
      for the LORD our God is the Holy One.

100

1 Be joyful in the LORD, all you lands; *
   serve the LORD with gladness
      and come before God's presence with a song.

2 Know this: The LORD alone is God; *
   we belong to the LORD, who made us;
      we are God's people and the sheep of God's pasture.

3 Enter God's gates with thanksgiving;
   go into the holy courts with praise; *
      give thanks and call upon the name of the LORD.

4 For good is the LORD,
   whose mercy is everlasting; *
      and whose faithfulness endures from age to age.

101

1 I will sing of mercy and justice; *
　　to you, O LORD, will I sing praises.

2 I will strive to follow a blameless course;
　oh, when will you come to me? *
　　I will walk with sincerity of heart within my house.

3 I will set no worthless thing before my eyes; *
　　I hate the doers of evil deeds;
　　they shall not remain with me.

4 A crooked heart shall be far from me; *
　　I will not know evil.

5 Those who in secret slander their neighbors I will destroy; *
　　those who have a haughty look and a proud heart I cannot abide.

6 My eyes are upon the faithful in the land, that they may dwell
　　with me, *
　　and only those who lead a blameless life shall be my servants.

7 Those who act deceitfully shall not dwell in my house, *
　　and those who tell lies shall not continue in my sight.

8 I will soon destroy all the wicked in the land, *
　　that I may root out all evildoers from the city of the LORD.

102

1 LORD, hear my prayer, and let my cry come before you; *
　　hide not your face from me in the day of my trouble.

2 Incline your ear to me; *
　　when I call, make haste to answer me,

3 For my days drift away like smoke, *
　　and my bones are hot as burning coals.

4 My heart is smitten like grass and withered, *
　　so that I forget to eat my bread.

5 Because of the voice of my groaning *
　　I am but skin and bones.

6 I have become like a vulture in the wilderness, *
   like an owl among the ruins.

7 I lie awake and groan; *
   I am like a sparrow, lonely on a house-top.

8 My enemies revile me all day long, *
   and those who scoff at me have taken an oath against me.

9 For I have eaten ashes for bread *
   and mingled my drink with weeping.

10 Because of your indignation and wrath *
    you have lifted me up and thrown me away.

11 My days pass away like a shadow, *
    and I wither like the grass.

12 But you, O Lord, endure for ever, *
    and your name from age to age.

13 You will arise and have compassion on Zion,
    for it is time to have mercy upon it; *
    indeed, the appointed time has come.

14 For your servants love its very rubble, *
    and are moved to pity even for its dust.

15 The nations shall fear your name, O Lord, *
    and all the rulers of the earth your glory.

16 For you, O Lord, will build up Zion, *
    and your glory will appear.

17 You will look with favor on the prayer of the homeless; *
    you will not despise their plea.

18 Let this be written for a future generation, *
    so that a people yet unborn may praise the Lord.

19 For the Lord looked down from the holy place on high *
    and from the heavens beheld the earth;

20 To hear the groan of the captive *
    and to set free those condemned to die;

21 That they may declare in Zion the name of the LORD, *
    and the praise of our God in Jerusalem;

22 When the peoples are gathered together, *
    and the realms also, to serve the LORD.

23 The LORD has brought down my strength before my time *
    and shortened the number of my days;

24 And I said, "O my God,
    do not take me away in the midst of my days; *
    your years endure throughout all generations.

25 In the beginning, O LORD, you laid the foundations of the earth, *
    and the heavens are the work of your hands;

26 They shall perish, but you will endure;
    they all shall wear out like a garment; *
      as clothing you will change them,
      and they shall be changed;

27 But you are always the same, *
    and your years will never end.

28 The children of your servants shall continue, *
    and their offspring shall stand fast in your sight."

103

1 Bless the LORD, O my soul, *
    and all that is within me, bless God's holy name.

2 Bless the LORD, O my soul, *
    and forget not all the benefits of the LORD,

3 Who forgives all your sins *
    and heals all your infirmities;

4 Who redeems your life from the grave *
    and crowns you with mercy and loving-kindness;

5 Who satisfies you with good things, *
    and your youth is renewed like an eagle's.

6 The LORD executes righteousness *
and judgment for all who are oppressed.

7 To Moses were made known God's ways *
and to the children of Israel the works of the LORD.

8 The LORD is full of compassion and mercy, *
slow to anger and of great kindness.

9 The LORD will not always accuse us *
nor remain angry for ever.

10 The LORD has not dealt with us according to our sins, *
nor rewarded us according to our wickedness.

11 For as the heavens are high above the earth, *
so is the LORD's mercy great upon the God-fearing.

12 As far as the east is from the west, *
so far has the LORD removed our sins from us.

13 As a father cares for his children, *
so does the LORD care for the God-fearing.

14 For the LORD knows whereof we are made *
and remembers that we are but dust.

15 Our days are like the grass; *
we flourish like a flower of the field;

16 When the wind goes over it, it is gone, *
and its place shall know it no more.

17 But the merciful goodness of the LORD endures for ever on the
God-fearing, *
and the righteousness of the LORD on children's children;

18 On those who keep the holy covenant *
and remember the commandments and do them.

19 The LORD has set up a throne in heaven, *
and the sovereignty of the LORD has dominion over all.

20 Bless the LORD, you holy angels,
you mighty ones who do God's bidding, *
and hearken to the voice of God's word.

21 Bless the Lᴏʀᴅ, all you holy hosts, *
    you holy ministers who do God's will.

22 Bless the Lᴏʀᴅ, all you works of God,
    in all places of God's dominion; *
    bless the Lᴏʀᴅ, O my soul.

104

1 Bless the Lᴏʀᴅ, O my soul; *
    O Lᴏʀᴅ my God, how excellent is your greatness!
    you are clothed with majesty and splendor.

2 You wrap yourself with light as with a cloak *
    and spread out the heavens like a curtain.

3 You lay the beams of your chambers in the waters above; *
    you make the clouds your chariot;
    you ride on the wings of the wind.

4 You make the winds your messengers *
    and flames of fire your servants.

5 You have set the earth upon its foundations, *
    so that it never shall move at any time.

6 You covered it with the deep as with a mantle; *
    the waters stood higher than the mountains.

7 At your rebuke they fled; *
    at the voice of your thunder they hastened away.

8 They went up into the hills and down to the valleys beneath, *
    to the places you had appointed for them.

9 You set the limits that they should not pass; *
    they shall not again cover the earth.

10 You send the springs into the valleys; *
    they flow between the mountains.

11 All the beasts of the field drink their fill from them, *
    and the wild asses quench their thirst.

12 Beside them the birds of the air make their nests *
   and sing among the branches.

13 You water the mountains from your dwelling on high; *
   the earth is fully satisfied by the fruit of your works.

14 You make grass grow for flocks and herds *
   and plants to serve humankind;

15 That they may bring forth food from the earth, *
   and wine to gladden our hearts,

16 Oil to make a cheerful countenance, *
   and bread to strengthen the heart.

17 The trees of the LORD are full of sap, *
   the cedars of Lebanon which the LORD planted,

18 In which the birds build their nests, *
   and in whose tops the stork makes its dwelling.

19 The high hills are a refuge for the mountain goats, *
   and the stony cliffs for the rock badgers.

20 You appointed the moon to mark the seasons, *
   and the sun knows the time of its setting.

21 You make darkness that it may be night, *
   in which all the beasts of the forest prowl.

22 The lions roar after their prey *
   and seek their food from God.

23 The sun rises, and they slip away *
   and lay themselves down in their dens.

24 Mortals go forth to their work *
   and to their labor until the evening.

25 O LORD, how manifold are your works! *
   in wisdom you have made them all;
   the earth is full of your creatures.

26 Yonder is the great and wide sea
   with its living things too many to number, *
   creatures both small and great.

27 There move the ships,
   and there is that Leviathan, *
      which you have made for the sport of it.

28 All of them look to you *
      to give them their food in due season.

29 You give it to them; they gather it; *
      you open your hand, and they are filled with good things.

30 You hide your face, and they are terrified; *
   you take away their breath,
      and they die and return to their dust.

31 You send forth your Spirit, and they are created; *
      and so you renew the face of the earth.

32 May your glory, O LORD, endure for ever; *
      may you rejoice in all your works.

33 You look at the earth and it trembles; *
      you touch the mountains and they smoke.

34 I will sing to the LORD as long as I live; *
      I will praise my God while I have my being.

35 May these words of mine please you; *
      I will rejoice in the LORD.

36 Let sinners be consumed out of the earth, *
      and the wicked be no more.

37 Bless the LORD, O my soul. *
   Hallelujah!

105

1 Give thanks to the LORD and call upon God's name; *
      make known the deeds of the LORD among the peoples.

2 Sing to the LORD, sing praises, *
      and speak of all God's marvelous works.

3 Glory in God's holy name; *
      let the hearts of those who seek the LORD rejoice.

4 Search for the LORD and the strength of the LORD; *
   continually seek the face of God.

5 Remember the marvels God has done, *
   the wonders and the judgments of God's mouth,

6 O offspring of Abraham, God's servant, *
   O children of Jacob, God's chosen.

7 The LORD is our God, *
   whose judgments prevail in all the world.

8 The LORD has always been mindful of the covenant, *
   the promise made for a thousand generations:

9 The covenant made with Abraham, *
   the oath sworn to Isaac,

10 Which God established as a statute for Jacob, *
   an everlasting covenant for Israel,

11 Saying, "To you will I give the land of Canaan *
   to be your allotted inheritance."

12 When they were few in number, *
   of little account, and sojourners in the land,

13 Wandering from nation to nation *
   and from one realm to another,

14 God let no one oppress them *
   and rebuked rulers for their sake,

15 Saying, "Do not touch my anointed *
   and do my prophets no harm."

16 Then the LORD called for a famine in the land *
   and destroyed the supply of bread.

17 The LORD sent a man before them, *
   Joseph, who was sold as a slave.

18 They bruised his feet in fetters; *
   his neck they put in an iron collar.

19 Until his prediction came to pass, *
    the word of the LORD tested him.

20 The king sent and released him; *
    the ruler of the peoples set him free.

21 He set him as a master over his household, *
    as a ruler over all his possessions,

22 To instruct his officials according to his will *
    and to teach his elders wisdom.

23 Israel came into Egypt, *
    and Jacob became a sojourner in the land of Ham.

24 The LORD made the chosen people exceedingly fruitful; *
    the LORD made them stronger than their enemies;

25 Whose heart God turned, so that they hated the chosen people, *
    and dealt unjustly with the servants of the LORD.

26 There came Moses, the servant of the LORD, *
    and Aaron whom God had chosen.

27 They worked signs from the LORD among them, *
    and portents in the land of Ham.

28 God sent darkness, and it grew dark; *
    but the Egyptians rebelled against the words of the LORD.

29 God turned their waters into blood *
    and caused their fish to die.

30 Their land was overrun by frogs, *
    in the very chambers of their rulers.

31 God spoke, and there came swarms of insects *
    and gnats within all their borders.

32 God gave them hailstones instead of rain, *
    and flames of fire throughout their land.

33 God blasted their vines and their fig trees *
    and shattered every tree in their country.

34 God spoke, and the locust came, *
   and young locusts without number,

35 Which ate up all the green plants in their land *
   and devoured the fruit of their soil.

36 God struck down the firstborn of their land, *
   the first fruits of all their strength.

37 God led out the chosen people with silver and gold; *
   in all their tribes there was not one that stumbled.

38 Egypt was glad of their going, *
   because they were afraid of them.

39 God spread out a cloud for a covering *
   and a fire to give light in the night season.

40 They asked, and quails appeared, *
   and God satisfied them with bread from heaven.

41 God opened the rock, and water flowed, *
   so the river ran in the dry places.

42 For God remembered the holy promise *
   and Abraham, chosen to serve.

43 So God led forth the people with gladness, *
   the chosen ones with shouts of joy.

44 God gave the chosen people the lands of the nations, *
   and they took the fruit of others' toil,

45 That they might keep God's statutes *
   and observe the laws of the Lord.
   Hallelujah!

106

1 Hallelujah!
   Give thanks to the Lord, who is good, *
   whose mercy endures for ever.

2 Can anyone declare the mighty acts of the Lord *
   or show forth all God's praise?

3 Happy are those who act with justice *
   and always do what is right!

4 Remember me, O Lord, with the favor you have for your people, *
   and visit me with your saving help;

5 That I may see the prosperity of your elect
   and be glad with the gladness of your people, *
   that I may glory with your inheritance.

6 We have sinned as our ancestors did; *
   we have done wrong and dealt wickedly.

7 In Egypt they did not consider your marvelous works,
   nor remember the abundance of your love; *
   they defied the Most High at the Red Sea.

8 But you saved them for your name's sake, *
   to make your power known.

9 The Lord rebuked the Red Sea, and it dried up; *
   God led them through the deep as through a desert.

10 The Lord saved them from the hand of those who hated them *
   and redeemed them from the hand of the enemy.

11 The waters covered their oppressors; *
   not one of them was left.

12 Then they believed the words of the Lord *
   and sang out songs of praise.

13 But they soon forgot the deeds of the Lord *
   and did not await divine counsel.

14 A craving seized them in the wilderness, *
   and they put God to the test in the desert.

15 God gave them what they asked, *
   but sent leanness into their soul.

16 They envied Moses in the camp, *
   and Aaron, the holy one of the Lord.

17 The earth opened and swallowed Dathan *
   and covered the company of Abiram.

18 Fire blazed up against their company, *
   and flames devoured the wicked.

19 Israel made a bull-calf at Horeb *
   and worshiped a molten image;

20 And so they exchanged their glory *
   for the image of an ox that feeds on grass.

21 They forgot God their Savior, *
   who had done great things in Egypt,

22 Wonderful deeds in the land of Ham, *
   and fearful things at the Red Sea.

23 So God would have destroyed them,
   had not Moses, the chosen one, stood before God in the breach, *
   to turn away divine wrath from consuming them.

24 They refused the pleasant land *
   and would not believe God's promise.

25 They grumbled in their tents *
   and would not listen to the voice of the LORD.

26 So God's hand was lifted against them, *
   to overthrow them in the wilderness,

27 To cast out their seed among the nations, *
   and to scatter them throughout the lands.

28 They joined themselves to Baal-Peor *
   and ate sacrifices offered to the dead.

29 They provoked the LORD to anger with their actions, *
   and a plague broke out among them.

30 Then Phinehas stood up and interceded, *
   and the plague came to an end.

31 This was reckoned to Phinehas as righteousness *
   throughout all generations for ever.

32 Again they provoked God's anger at the waters of Meribah, *
   and the LORD punished Moses because of them;

33 For they so embittered his spirit *
   that he spoke rash words with his lips.

34 They did not destroy the peoples *
   as the LORD had commanded them.

35 They intermingled with the heathen *
   and learned their pagan ways,

36 So that they worshiped their idols, *
   which became a snare to them.

37 They sacrificed their sons *
   and their daughters to evil spirits.

38 They shed innocent blood,
   the blood of their sons and daughters, *
      which they offered to the idols of Canaan,
      and the land was defiled with blood.

39 Thus they were polluted by their actions *
   and went whoring in their evil deeds.

40 Therefore the wrath of the LORD was kindled against the people *
   and God abhorred the chosen inheritance.

41 God gave them over to the hand of the heathen, *
   and those who hated them ruled over them.

42 Their enemies oppressed them, *
   and they were humbled under their hand.

43 Many a time did God deliver them,
   but they rebelled through their own devices, *
      and were brought down in their iniquity.

44 Nevertheless, the LORD saw their distress *
   and heard their lamentation.

45 God remembered the covenant with them *
   and out of abundant mercy relented.

46 God caused them to be pitied *
   by those who held them captive.

47 Save us, O LORD our God,
    and gather us from among the nations, *
        that we may give thanks to your holy name
        and glory in your praise.

48 Blessed be the LORD, the God of Israel,
    from everlasting and to everlasting; *
        and let all the people say, "Amen!"
    Hallelujah!

107

1 Give thanks to the LORD, who is good, *
    whose mercy endures for ever.

2 Let all those whom the LORD has redeemed proclaim *
    that the LORD redeemed them from the hand of the foe.

3 God gathered them out of the lands; *
    from the east and from the west,
    from the north and from the south.

4 Some wandered in desert wastes; *
    they found no way to a city where they might dwell.

5 They were hungry and thirsty; *
    their spirits languished within them.

6 Then in their trouble they cried to the LORD, *
    who delivered them from their distress.

7 The LORD put their feet on a straight path *
    to go to a city where they might dwell.

8 Let them give thanks for the mercy of God, *
    for the wonders the LORD does for all people.

9 For God satisfies the thirsty *
    and fills the hungry with good things.

10 Some sat in darkness and deep gloom, *
    bound fast in misery and iron;

11 Because they rebelled against the words of God *
    and despised the counsel of the Most High.

12 So God humbled their spirits with hard labor; *
    they stumbled, and there was none to help.

13 Then in their trouble they cried to the LORD, *
    who delivered them from their distress.

14 The LORD led them out of darkness and deep gloom *
    and broke their bonds asunder.

15 Let them give thanks for the mercy of God, *
    for the wonders the LORD does for all people.

16 For God shatters the doors of bronze *
    and breaks in two the iron bars.

17 Some were fools and took to rebellious ways; *
    they were afflicted because of their sins.

18 They abhorred all manner of food *
    and drew near to death's door.

19 Then in their trouble they cried to the LORD, *
    who delivered them from their distress.

20 God sent forth a word to heal them *
    and saved them from the grave.

21 Let them give thanks for the mercy of God, *
    for the wonders the LORD does for all people.

22 Let them offer a sacrifice of thanksgiving *
    and recount the deeds of God with shouts of joy.

23 Some went down to the sea in ships *
    and plied their trade in deep waters;

24 They beheld the works of the LORD, *
    whose wonders are in the deep.

25 Then the LORD spoke, and a stormy wind arose, *
    which tossed high the waves of the sea.

26 They mounted up to the heavens and fell back to the depths; *
    their hearts melted because of their peril.

27 They reeled and staggered like drunkards *
    and were at their wits' end.

28 Then in their trouble they cried to the LORD, *
    who delivered them from their distress.

29 God stilled the storm to a whisper *
    and quieted the waves of the sea.

30 Then were they glad because of the calm, *
    and God brought them to the harbor they were bound for.

31 Let them give thanks for the mercy of God, *
    for the wonders the LORD does for all people.

32 Let them exalt the LORD in the congregation of the people *
    and praise God in the council of the elders.

33 The LORD changed rivers into deserts, *
    and water-springs into thirsty ground,

34 A fruitful land into salt flats, *
    because of the wickedness of those who dwell there.

35 God changed deserts into pools of water *
    and dry land into water-springs.

36 God settled the hungry there, *
    and they founded a city to dwell in.

37 They sowed fields, and planted vineyards, *
    and brought in a fruitful harvest.

38 God blessed them, so that they increased greatly; *
    God did not let their herds decrease.

39 Yet when they were diminished and brought low, *
    through stress of adversity and sorrow,

40 (God pours contempt on nobles *
    and makes them wander in trackless wastes)

41 God lifted up the poor out of misery *
    and multiplied their families like flocks of sheep.

42 The upright will see this and rejoice, *
   but all wickedness will shut its mouth.

43 Whoever is wise will ponder these things, *
   and consider well the mercies of the LORD.

108

1 My heart is firmly fixed, O God, my heart is fixed; *
   I will sing and make melody.

2 Wake up, my spirit;
   awake, lute and harp; *
   I myself will waken the dawn.

3 I will confess you among the peoples, O LORD; *
   I will sing praises to you among the nations.

4 For your loving-kindness is greater than the heavens, *
   and your faithfulness reaches to the clouds.

5 Exalt yourself above the heavens, O God, *
   and your glory over all the earth.

6 So that those who are dear to you may be delivered, *
   save with your right hand and answer me.

7 From God's holy place came a voice; *
   God said, "I will exult and parcel out Shechem;
   I will divide the valley of Succoth.

8 Gilead is mine and Manasseh is mine; *
   Ephraim is my helmet and Judah my scepter.

9 Moab is my washbasin,
   on Edom I throw down my sandal to claim it, *
   and over Philistia will I shout in triumph."

10 Who will lead me into the strong city? *
   who will bring me into Edom?

11 Have you not cast us off, O God? *
   you no longer go out, O God, with our armies.

12 Grant us your help against the enemy, *
    for vain is the help of mortals.

13 With God we will do valiant deeds, *
    and God shall tread our enemies under foot.

109

1 Hold not your tongue, O God of my praise; *
   for the mouth of the wicked,
   the mouth of the deceitful, is opened against me.

2 They speak to me with a lying tongue; *
   they encompass me with hateful words
   and fight against me without a cause.

3 Despite my love, they accuse me; *
   but as for me, I pray for them.

4 They repay evil for good, *
   and hatred for my love.

5 They set the wicked against me, *
   and let an accuser stand at my right hand.

6 When they judge me, they find me guilty; *
   my appeal is in vain.

7 They say, "Let your days be few, *
   and let another take your office.

8 Let your children be orphaned, *
   and your spouse bereft.

9 Let your children be waifs and beggars; *
   let them be driven from the ruins of their homes.

10 Let the creditor seize everything you have; *
    let strangers plunder your gains.

11 Let there be no one to show you kindness, *
    and none to pity your orphaned children.

12 Let your descendants be destroyed, *
    and your name be blotted out in the next generation.

13 Let the wickedness of your fathers be remembered before the
       LORD, *
     and your mother's sin not be blotted out;

14 Let their sin be always before the LORD; *
     but let the LORD root out their names from the earth;

15 Because you did not remember to show mercy, *
     but persecuted the poor and needy
     and sought to kill the brokenhearted.

16 You loved cursing,
     let it come upon you; *
       you took no delight in blessing,
       let it depart from you.

17 You put on cursing like a garment, *
     let it soak into your body like water
     and into your bones like oil;

18 Let it be to you like the cloak which you
     wrap around yourself, *
       and like the belt that you wear continually.''

19 O LORD, let this fate be your recompense to my accusers, *
     and to those who speak evil against me.

20 But you, O Lord my GOD,
     oh, deal with me according to your name; *
       for your tender mercy's sake, deliver me.

21 For I am poor and needy, *
     and my heart is wounded within me.

22 I have faded away like a shadow when it lengthens; *
     I am shaken off like a locust.

23 My knees are weak through fasting, *
     and my flesh is wasted and gaunt.

24 I have become a reproach to them; *
     they see and shake their heads.

25 Help me, O LORD my God; *
     save me for your mercy's sake.

26 Let them know that this is your hand, *
    that you, O LORD, have done it.

27 They may curse, but you will bless; *
    let those who rise up against me be put to shame,
    and your servant will rejoice.

28 Let my accusers be clothed with disgrace *
    and wrap themselves in their shame as in a cloak.

29 I will give great thanks to you, O LORD, with my mouth; *
    in the midst of the multitude will I praise you;

30 Because you stand at the right hand of the needy, *
    to save their life from those who would condemn them.

110

1 The LORD said to my lord, "Sit at my right hand, *
    until I make your enemies your footstool."

2 The LORD will send the scepter of your power out of Zion, *
    saying, "Rule over your enemies round about you.

3 Nobility has been yours from the day of your birth; *
    in the beauty of holiness have I begotten you,
    like dew from the womb of the morning."

4 The LORD has sworn and will not recant: *
    "You are a priest for ever after the order of Melchizedek."

5 The lord who is at God's right hand
    will smite rulers in the day of his wrath; *
    he will rule over the nations.

6 He will heap high the corpses *
    and will smash heads over the wide earth.

7 He will drink from the brook beside the road *
    and therefore will lift high his head.

111

1 Hallelujah!
   I will give thanks to the LORD with my whole heart, *
      in the assembly of the upright, in the congregation.

2 Great are the deeds of the LORD! *
      they are studied by all who delight in them.

3 Full of majesty and splendor is the work of the LORD, *
      whose righteousness endures for ever.

4 Gracious and full of compassion is the LORD, *
      whose marvelous works are to be remembered.

5 The LORD gives food to the God-fearing, *
      ever mindful of the covenant.

6 The LORD has shown the chosen people works of power *
      in giving them the lands of the nations.

7 The hands of the LORD work faithfulness and justice; *
      all the commandments of the LORD are sure.

8 They stand fast for ever and ever, *
      because they are done in truth and equity.

9 The LORD sent redemption to the chosen people,
   commanding the covenant for ever; *
      holy and awesome is the name of the LORD.

10 The fear of the LORD is the beginning of wisdom; *
      those who act accordingly have a good understanding;
      the praise of the LORD endures for ever.

112

1 Hallelujah!
   Happy are they who fear the LORD *
      and have great delight in the LORD's commandments!

2 Their descendants will be mighty in the land; *
      the generation of the upright will be blessed.

3 Wealth and riches will be in their house, *
   and their righteousness will last for ever.

4 Light shines in the darkness for the upright; *
   the righteous are merciful and full of compassion.

5 It is good for them to be generous in lending *
   and to manage their affairs with justice.

6 For they will never be shaken; *
   the righteous will be kept in everlasting remembrance.

7 They will not be afraid of any evil rumors; *
   their heart is right;
   they put their trust in the LORD.

8 Their heart is established and will not shrink, *
   until they see their desire upon their enemies.

9 They have given freely to the poor, *
   and their righteousness stands fast for ever;
   they will hold up their head with honor.

10 The wicked will see it and be angry;
   they will gnash their teeth and pine away; *
   the desires of the wicked will perish.

113

1 Hallelujah!
   Give praise, you servants of the LORD; *
   praise the name of the LORD.

2 Let the name of the LORD be blessed, *
   from this time forth for evermore.

3 From the rising of the sun to its going down *
   let the name of the LORD be praised.

4 High above all nations is the LORD, *
   whose glory is above the heavens.

5 Who is like the LORD our God, who sits enthroned on high *
   but stoops to behold the heavens and the earth?

6 The LORD takes up the weak out of the dust *
   and lifts up the poor from the ashes.

7 The LORD sets them with the nobles, *
   with the nobles of the chosen people.

8 The LORD makes the woman of a childless house *
   to be a joyful mother of children.

114

1 Hallelujah!
   When Israel came out of Egypt, *
      the house of Jacob from a people of strange speech,

2 Judah became God's sanctuary *
   and Israel God's dominion.

3 The sea beheld it and fled; *
   Jordan turned and went back.

4 The mountains skipped like rams, *
   and the little hills like young sheep.

5 What ailed you, O sea, that you fled? *
   O Jordan, that you turned back?

6 You mountains, that you skipped like rams? *
   you little hills like young sheep?

7 Tremble, O earth, at the presence of the Lord, *
   at the presence of the God of Jacob,

8 Who turned the hard rock into a pool of water *
   and flint-stone into a flowing spring.

115

1 Not to us, O LORD, not to us,
   but to your name give glory; *
      because of your love and because of your faithfulness.

2 Why should the heathen say, *
   "Where then is their God?"

3 Our God is in heaven; *
     whatever God wills to do, God does.

4 Their idols are silver and gold, *
     the work of human hands.

5 They have mouths, but they cannot speak; *
     eyes have they, but they cannot see;

6 They have ears, but they cannot hear; *
     noses, but they cannot smell;

7 They have hands, but they cannot feel;
   feet, but they cannot walk; *
     they make no sound with their throat.

8 Those who make them are like them, *
     and so are all who put their trust in them.

9 O Israel, trust in the LORD, *
     who is your help and your shield.

10 O house of Aaron, trust in the LORD, *
     who is your help and your shield.

11 You who fear the LORD, trust in the LORD, *
     who is your help and your shield.

12 The LORD has been mindful of us and will bless us; *
     the LORD will bless the house of Israel
     and will bless the house of Aaron;

13 The LORD will bless the God-fearing, *
     both small and great together.

14 May the LORD increase you more and more, *
     you and your children after you.

15 May you be blessed by the LORD, *
     the maker of heaven and earth.

16 The heaven of heavens is the LORD's, *
     but the LORD entrusted the earth to its peoples.

17 The dead do not praise the LORD, *
     nor all those who go down into silence;

18 But we will bless the LORD, *
   from this time forth for evermore.
   Hallelujah!

116

1 I love the LORD, because the LORD has heard the voice of my
      supplication *
   and inclined an ear to me whenever I cried out.

2 The cords of death entangled me;
   the grip of the grave took hold of me; *
   I came to grief and sorrow.

3 Then I called upon the name of the LORD: *
   "O LORD, I pray you, save my life."

4 Gracious is the LORD and righteous; *
   our God is full of compassion.

5 The LORD watches over the innocent; *
   I was brought very low, and the LORD helped me.

6 Turn again to your rest, O my soul, *
   for the LORD has treated you well.

7 For you have rescued my life from death, *
   my eyes from tears, and my feet from stumbling.

8 I will walk in the presence of the LORD *
   in the land of the living.

9 I believed, even when I said,
   "I have been brought very low." *
   In my distress I said, "No one can be trusted."

10 How shall I repay you, O LORD, *
   for all the good things you have done for me?

11 I will lift up the cup of salvation *
   and call upon the name of the LORD.

12 I will fulfill my vows to the LORD *
   in the presence of all the chosen people.

13 Precious in your sight, O Lord, *
     is the death of your servants.

14 O Lord, I am your servant; *
     I am your servant and the child of your handmaid;
     you have freed me from my bonds.

15 I will offer you the sacrifice of thanksgiving *
     and call upon the name of the Lord.

16 I will fulfill my vows to the Lord *
     in the presence of all the people,

17 In the courts of the Lord's house, *
     in the midst of you, O Jerusalem.
     Hallelujah!

117

1 Praise the Lord, all you nations; *
     give praise, all you peoples.

2 For the loving-kindness of the Lord toward us is great, *
     and the faithfulness of the Lord endures for ever.
     Hallelujah!

118

1 Give thanks to the Lord, who is good, *
     whose mercy endures for ever.

2 Let Israel now proclaim, *
     "The mercy of the Lord endures for ever."

3 Let the house of Aaron now proclaim, *
     "The mercy of the Lord endures for ever."

4 Let those who fear the Lord now proclaim, *
     "The mercy of the Lord endures for ever."

5 I called to the Lord in my distress; *
     the Lord answered by setting me free.

6 The Lord is at my side, therefore I will not fear; *
     what can anyone do to me?

7 The LORD is at my side to help me; *
   I will triumph over those who hate me.

8 It is better to rely on the LORD *
   than to put any trust in flesh.

9 It is better to rely on the LORD *
   than to put any trust in rulers.

10 All the ungodly encompass me; *
   in the name of the LORD I will repel them.

11 They hem me in, they hem me in on every side; *
   in the name of the LORD I will repel them.

12 They swarm about me like bees;
   they blaze like a fire of thorns; *
   in the name of the LORD I will repel them.

13 I was pressed so hard that I almost fell, *
   but the LORD came to my help.

14 The LORD is my strength and my song *
   and has become my salvation.

15 There is a sound of exultation and victory *
   in the tents of the righteous:

16 "The right hand of the LORD has triumphed! *
   the right hand of the LORD is exalted!
   the right hand of the LORD has triumphed!"

17 I shall not die, but live, *
   and declare the works of the LORD.

18 The LORD has punished me sorely *
   but did not hand me over to death.

19 Open for me the gates of righteousness; *
   I will enter them;
   I will offer thanks to the LORD.

20 "This is the gate of the LORD; *
   those who are righteous may enter."

21 I will give thanks to you, for you answered me *
and have become my salvation.

22 The same stone which the builders rejected *
has become the chief cornerstone.

23 This is the LORD's doing, *
and it is marvelous in our eyes.

24 On this day the LORD has acted; *
we will rejoice and be glad in it.

25 Hosannah, LORD, hosannah! *
LORD, send us now success.

26 Blessed is the one who comes in the name of the LORD; *
we bless you from the house of the LORD.

27 God is the LORD, who has shined upon us; *
form a procession with branches up to the horns of
the altar.

28 "You are my God, and I will thank you; *
you are my God, and I will exalt you."

29 Give thanks to the LORD, who is good, *
whose mercy endures for ever.

119 Aleph

1 Happy are they whose way is blameless, *
who walk in the law of the LORD!

2 Happy are they who observe your decrees *
and seek you with all their hearts!

3 Who never do any wrong, *
but always walk in your ways.

4 You laid down your commandments, *
that we should fully keep them.

5 Oh, that my ways were made so direct *
that I might keep your statutes!

6 Then I should not be put to shame, *
  when I regard all your commandments.

7 I will thank you with an unfeigned heart, *
  when I have learned your righteous judgments.

8 I will keep your statutes; *
  do not utterly forsake me.

Beth

9 How shall the young cleanse their way? *
  By keeping to your words.

10 With my whole heart I seek you; *
   let me not stray from your commandments.

11 I treasure your promise in my heart, *
   that I may not sin against you.

12 Blessed are you, O LORD; *
   instruct me in your statutes.

13 With my lips will I recite *
   all the judgments of your mouth.

14 I have taken greater delight in the way of your decrees *
   than in all manner of riches.

15 I will meditate on your commandments *
   and give attention to your ways.

16 My delight is in your statutes; *
   I will not forget your word.

Gimel

17 Deal bountifully with your servant, *
   that I may live and keep your word.

18 Open my eyes, that I may see *
   the wonders of your law.

19 I am a stranger here on earth; *
   do not hide your commandments from me.

20 My soul is consumed at all times *
    with longing for your judgments.

21 You have rebuked the insolent; *
    cursed are they who stray from your commandments!

22 Turn from me shame and rebuke, *
    for I have kept your decrees.

23 Even though rulers sit and plot against me, *
    I will meditate on your statutes.

24 For your decrees are my delight, *
    and they are my counselors.

Daleth

25 My soul cleaves to the dust; *
    give me life according to your word.

26 I have confessed my ways, and you answered me; *
    instruct me in your statutes.

27 Make me understand the way of your commandments, *
    that I may meditate on your marvelous works.

28 My soul melts away for sorrow; *
    strengthen me according to your word.

29 Take from me the way of lying; *
    let me find grace through your law.

30 I have chosen the way of faithfulness; *
    I have set your judgments before me.

31 I hold fast to your decrees; *
    O Lord, let me not be put to shame.

32 I will run the way of your commandments, *
    for you have set my heart at liberty.

He

33 Teach me, O Lord, the way of your statutes, *
    and I shall keep it to the end.

34 Give me understanding, and I shall keep your law; *
    I shall keep it with all my heart.

35 Make me go in the path of your commandments, *
    for that is my desire.

36 Incline my heart to your decrees *
    and not to unjust gain.

37 Turn my eyes from watching what is worthless; *
    give me life in your ways.

38 Fulfill your promise to your servant, *
    which you make to those who fear you.

39 Turn away the reproach which I dread, *
    because your judgments are good.

40 Behold, I long for your commandments; *
    in your righteousness preserve my life.

Waw

41 Let your loving-kindness come to me, O LORD, *
    and your salvation, according to your promise.

42 Then shall I have a word for those who taunt me, *
    because I trust in your words.

43 Do not take the word of truth out of my mouth, *
    for my hope is in your judgments.

44 I shall continue to keep your law; *
    I shall keep it for ever and ever.

45 I will walk at liberty, *
    because I study your commandments.

46 I will tell of your decrees before rulers *
    and will not be ashamed.

47 I delight in your commandments, *
    which I have always loved.

48 I will lift up my hands to your commandments, *
    and I will meditate on your statutes.

Zayin

49 Remember your word to your servant, *
   because you have given me hope.

50 This is my comfort in my trouble, *
   that your promise gives me life.

51 The proud have derided me cruelly, *
   but I have not turned from your law.

52 When I remember your judgments of old, *
   O LORD, I take great comfort.

53 I am filled with a burning rage, *
   because of the wicked who forsake your law.

54 Your statutes have been like songs to me *
   wherever I have lived as a stranger.

55 I remember your name in the night, O LORD, *
   and dwell upon your law.

56 This is how it has been with me, *
   because I have kept your commandments.

Heth

57 You only are my portion, O LORD; *
   I have promised to keep your words.

58 I entreat you with all my heart, *
   be merciful to me according to your promise.

59 I have considered my ways *
   and turned my feet toward your decrees.

60 I hasten and do not tarry *
   to keep your commandments.

61 Though the cords of the wicked entangle me, *
   I do not forget your law.

62 At midnight I will rise to give you thanks, *
   because of your righteous judgments.

63 I am a companion of all who fear you; *
    and of those who keep your commandments.

64 The earth, O LORD, is full of your love; *
    instruct me in your statutes.

Teth

65 O LORD, you have dealt graciously with your servant, *
    according to your word.

66 Teach me discernment and knowledge, *
    for I have believed in your commandments.

67 Before I was afflicted I went astray, *
    but now I keep your word.

68 You are good and you bring forth good; *
    instruct me in your statutes.

69 The proud have smeared me with lies, *
    but I will keep your commandments with my whole heart.

70 Their heart is gross and fat, *
    but my delight is in your law.

71 It is good for me that I have been afflicted, *
    that I might learn your statutes.

72 The law of your mouth is dearer to me *
    than thousands in gold and silver.

Yodh

73 Your hands have made me and fashioned me; *
    give me understanding, that I may learn your commandments.

74 Those who fear you will be glad when they see me, *
    because I trust in your word.

75 I know, O LORD, that your judgments are right *
    and that in faithfulness you have afflicted me.

76 Let your loving-kindness be my comfort, *
    as you have promised to your servant.

77 Let your compassion come to me, that I may live, *
   for your law is my delight.

78 Let the arrogant be put to shame, for they wrong me with lies; *
   but I will meditate on your commandments.

79 Let those who fear you turn to me, *
   and also those who know your decrees.

80 Let my heart be sound in your statutes, *
   that I may not be put to shame.

Kaph

81 My soul has longed for your salvation; *
   I have put my hope in your word.

82 My eyes have failed from watching for your promise, *
   and I say, "When will you comfort me?"

83 I have become like a leather flask in the smoke, *
   but I have not forgotten your statutes.

84 How much longer must I wait? *
   when will you give judgment against those who persecute me?

85 The proud have dug pits for me; *
   they do not keep your law.

86 All your commandments are true; *
   help me, for they persecute me with lies.

87 They had almost made an end of me on earth, *
   but I have not forsaken your commandments.

88 In your loving-kindness, revive me, *
   that I may keep the decrees of your mouth.

Lamedh

89 O LORD, your word is everlasting; *
   it stands firm in the heavens.

90 Your faithfulness remains from one generation to another; *
   you established the earth, and it abides.

91 By your decree these continue to this day, *
    for all things are your servants.

92 If my delight had not been in your law, *
    I should have perished in my affliction.

93 I will never forget your commandments, *
    because by them you give me life.

94 I am yours; oh, that you would save me! *
    for I study your commandments.

95 Though the wicked lie in wait for me to destroy me, *
    I will apply my mind to your decrees.

96 I see that all things come to an end, *
    but your commandment has no bounds.

Mem

97 Oh, how I love your law! *
    all the day long it is in my mind.

98 Your commandment has made me wiser than my enemies, *
    and it is always with me.

99 I have more understanding than all my teachers, *
    for your decrees are my study.

100 I am wiser than the elders, *
    because I observe your commandments.

101 I restrain my feet from every evil way, *
    that I may keep your word.

102 I do not shrink from your judgments, *
    because you yourself have taught me.

103 How sweet are your words to my taste! *
    they are sweeter than honey to my mouth.

104 Through your commandments I gain understanding; *
    therefore I hate every lying way.

Nun

105 Your word is a lantern to my feet *
    and a light upon my path.

106 I have sworn and am determined *
    to keep your righteous judgments.

107 I am deeply troubled; *
    preserve my life, O LORD, according to your word.

108 Accept, O LORD, the willing tribute of my lips, *
    and teach me your judgments.

109 My life is always in my hand, *
    yet I do not forget your law.

110 The wicked have set a trap for me, *
    but I have not strayed from your commandments.

111 Your decrees are my inheritance for ever; *
    truly, they are the joy of my heart.

112 I have applied my heart to fulfill your statutes *
    for ever and to the end.

Samekh

113 I hate those who have a divided heart, *
    but your law do I love.

114 You are my refuge and shield; *
    my hope is in your word.

115 Away from me, you wicked! *
    I will keep the commandments of my God.

116 Sustain me according to your promise, that I may live, *
    and let me not be disappointed in my hope.

117 Hold me up, and I shall be safe, *
    and my delight shall be ever in your statutes.

118 You spurn all who stray from your statutes; *
    their deceitfulness is in vain.

119 In your sight all the wicked of the earth are but dross; *
    therefore I love your decrees.

120 My flesh trembles with dread of you; *
    I am afraid of your judgments.

Ayin

121 I have done what is just and right; *
    do not deliver me to my oppressors.

122 Be surety for your servant's good; *
    let not the proud oppress me.

123 My eyes have failed from watching for your salvation *
    and for your righteous promise.

124 Deal with your servant according to your loving-kindness *
    and teach me your statutes.

125 I am your servant; grant me understanding, *
    that I may know your decrees.

126 It is time for you to act, O LORD, *
    for they have broken your law.

127 Truly, I love your commandments *
    more than gold and precious stones.

128 I hold all your commandments to be right for me; *
    all paths of falsehood I abhor.

Pe

129 Your decrees are wonderful; *
    therefore I obey them with all my heart.

130 When your word goes forth it gives light; *
    it gives understanding to the simple.

131 I open my mouth and pant; *
    I long for your commandments.

132 Turn to me in mercy, *
    as you always do to those who love your name.

133 Steady my footsteps in your word; *
  let no iniquity have dominion over me.

134 Rescue me from those who oppress me, *
  and I will keep your commandments.

135 Let your countenance shine upon your servant *
  and teach me your statutes.

136 My eyes shed streams of tears, *
  because people do not keep your law.

Sadhe

137 You are righteous, O Lord, *
  and upright are your judgments.

138 You have issued your decrees *
  with justice and in perfect faithfulness.

139 My indignation has consumed me, *
  because my enemies forget your words.

140 Your word has been tested to the uttermost, *
  and your servant holds it dear.

141 I am small and of little account, *
  yet I do not forget your commandments.

142 Your justice is an everlasting justice *
  and your law is the truth.

143 Trouble and distress have come upon me, *
  yet your commandments are my delight.

144 The righteousness of your decrees is everlasting; *
  grant me understanding, that I may live.

Qoph

145 I call with my whole heart; *
  answer me, O Lord, that I may keep your statutes.

146 I call to you;
oh, that you would save me! *
I will keep your decrees.

147 Early in the morning I cry out to you, *
for in your word is my trust.

148 My eyes are open in the night watches, *
that I may meditate upon your promise.

149 Hear my voice, O LORD, according to your loving-kindness; *
according to your judgments, give me life.

150 They draw near who in malice persecute me; *
they are very far from your law.

151 You, O LORD, are near at hand, *
and all your commandments are true.

152 Long have I known from your decrees *
that you have established them for ever.

Resh

153 Behold my affliction and deliver me, *
for I do not forget your law.

154 Plead my cause and redeem me; *
according to your promise, give me life.

155 Deliverance is far from the wicked, *
for they do not study your statutes.

156 Great is your compassion, O LORD; *
preserve my life, according to your judgments.

157 There are many who persecute and oppress me, *
yet I have not swerved from your decrees.

158 I look with loathing at the faithless, *
for they have not kept your word.

159 See how I love your commandments! *
O LORD, in your mercy, preserve me.

160 The heart of your word is truth; *
   all your righteous judgments endure for evermore.

Shin

161 Rulers have persecuted me without a cause, *
   but my heart stands in awe of your word.

162 I am as glad because of your promise *
   as one who finds great spoils.

163 As for lies, I hate and abhor them, *
   but your law is my love.

164 Seven times a day do I praise you, *
   because of your righteous judgments.

165 Great peace have they who love your law; *
   for them there is no stumbling block.

166 I have hoped for your salvation, O LORD, *
   and I have fulfilled your commandments.

167 I have kept your decrees *
   and I have loved them deeply.

168 I have kept your commandments and decrees, *
   for all my ways are before you.

Taw

169 Let my cry come before you, O LORD; *
   give me understanding, according to your word.

170 Let my supplication come before you; *
   deliver me, according to your promise.

171 My lips shall pour forth your praise, *
   when you teach me your statutes.

172 My tongue shall sing of your promise, *
   for all your commandments are righteous.

173 Let your hand be ready to help me, *
   for I have chosen your commandments.

174 I long for your salvation, O LORD, *
    and your law is my delight.

175 Let me live, and I will praise you, *
    and let your judgments help me.

176 I have gone astray like a sheep that is lost; *
    search for your servant,
    for I do not forget your commandments.

120

1 When I was in trouble, I called to the LORD; *
    I called to the LORD, who answered me.

2 Deliver me, O LORD, from lying lips *
    and from the deceitful tongue.

3 What shall be done to you, and what more besides, *
    O you deceitful tongue?

4 The sharpened arrows of a warrior, *
    along with hot glowing coals.

5 How hateful it is that I must lodge in Meshech *
    and dwell among the tents of Kedar!

6 Too long have I had to live *
    among the enemies of peace.

7 I am on the side of peace, *
    but when I speak of it, they are for war.

121

1 I lift up my eyes to the hills; *
    from where is my help to come?

2 My help comes from the LORD, *
    the maker of heaven and earth.

3 The LORD will not let your foot be moved, *
    and the One who watches over you will not fall asleep.

4 Behold, the One who keeps watch over Israel *
  shall neither slumber nor sleep;

5 It is the LORD who watches over you; *
  the LORD is your shade at your right hand,

6 So that the sun shall not strike you by day, *
  nor the moon by night.

7 The LORD shall preserve you from all evil; *
  the LORD shall keep you safe.

8 The LORD shall watch over your going out and your coming in, *
  from this time forth for evermore.

122

1 I was glad when they said to me, *
  "Let us go to the house of the LORD."

2 Now our feet are standing *
  within your gates, O Jerusalem.

3 Jerusalem is built as a city *
  that is at unity with itself;

4 To which the tribes go up,
  the tribes of the LORD, *
    the assembly of Israel,
    to praise the name of the LORD.

5 For there are the thrones of judgment, *
  the thrones of the house of David.

6 Pray for the peace of Jerusalem: *
  "May they prosper who love you.

7 Peace be within your walls *
  and quietness within your towers.

8 For the sake of my kindred and companions, *
  I pray for your prosperity.

9 Because of the house of the LORD our God, *
  I will seek to do you good."

123

1 To you I lift up my eyes, *
   to you enthroned in the heavens.

2 As the eyes of servants look to the hand of their masters, *
   and the eyes of a maid to the hand of her mistress,

3 So our eyes look to you, O Lᴏʀᴅ our God, *
   until you show us your mercy.

4 Have mercy upon us, O Lᴏʀᴅ, have mercy, *
   for we have had more than enough of contempt,

5 Too much of the scorn of the indolent rich, *
   and of the derision of the proud.

124

1 If the Lᴏʀᴅ had not been on our side, *
   let Israel now say;

2 If the Lᴏʀᴅ had not been on our side, *
   when enemies rose up against us;

3 Then would they have swallowed us up alive *
   in their fierce anger toward us;

4 Then would the waters have overwhelmed us *
   and the torrent gone over us;

5 Then would the raging waters *
   have gone right over us.

6 Blessed be the Lᴏʀᴅ, *
   who has not given us over to be a prey for their teeth.

7 We have escaped like a bird from the snare of the fowler; *
   the snare is broken, and we have escaped.

8 Our help is in the name of the Lᴏʀᴅ, *
   the maker of heaven and earth.

125

1 Those who trust in the LORD are like Mount Zion, *
   which cannot be moved, but stands fast for ever.

2 The hills stand about Jerusalem; *
   so does the LORD stand round about the chosen people,
   from this time forth for evermore.

3 The scepter of the wicked shall not hold sway over the land
      allotted to the just, *
   so that the just shall not put their hands to evil.

4 Show your goodness, O LORD, to those who are good *
   and to those who are true of heart.

5 As for those who turn aside to crooked ways,
   the LORD will lead them away with the evildoers; *
   but peace be upon Israel.

126

1 When the LORD restored the fortunes of Zion, *
   then were we like those who dream.

2 Then was our mouth filled with laughter, *
   and our tongue with shouts of joy.

3 Then they said among the nations, *
   "The LORD has done great things for them."

4 The LORD has done great things for us, *
   and we are glad indeed.

5 Restore our fortunes, O LORD, *
   like the watercourses of the Negev.

6 Those who sowed with tears *
   will reap with songs of joy.

7 Those who go out weeping, carrying the seed, *
   will come again with joy, shouldering their sheaves.

127

1 Unless the LORD builds the house, *
    their labor is in vain who build it.

2 Unless the LORD watches over the city, *
    in vain the sentries keep vigil.

3 It is in vain that you rise so early and go to bed so late; *
    vain, too, to eat the bread of toil,
    for to the beloved the LORD gives sleep.

4 Children are a heritage from the LORD, *
    and the fruit of the womb is a gift.

5 Like arrows in the hand of a warrior *
    are the children of one's youth.

6 Happy are the warriors with a quiver full of them! *
    they shall not be put to shame
    when they contend with their enemies in the gate.

128

1 Happy are they all who fear the LORD, *
    and who follow in the ways of the LORD!

2 You, O man, shall eat the fruit of your labor; *
    happiness and prosperity shall be yours.

3 Your wife shall be like a fruitful vine within your house, *
    your children like olive shoots round about your table.

4 The husband who fears the LORD *
    shall thus indeed be blessed.

5 The LORD bless you from Zion, *
    and may you see the prosperity of Jerusalem all the days of
        your life.

6 May you live to see your children's children; *
    may peace be upon Israel.

129

1 "Greatly have they oppressed me since my youth," *
   let Israel now say;

2 "Greatly have they oppressed me since my youth, *
   but they have not prevailed against me."

3 The plowers plowed upon my back *
   and made their furrows long.

4 The Lord, the Righteous One, *
   has cut the cords of the wicked.

5 Let them be put to shame and thrown back, *
   all those who are enemies of Zion.

6 Let them be like grass upon the housetops, *
   which withers before it can be plucked;

7 Which does not fill the hand of the reaper, *
   nor the bosom of those who bind the sheaves;

8 So that those who go by say not so much as,
   "The Lord prosper you. *
   We wish you well in the name of the Lord."

130

1 Out of the depths have I called to you, O Lord;
   Lord, hear my voice; *
   let your ears consider well the voice of my supplication.

2 If you, Lord, were to note what is done amiss, *
   O Lord, who could stand?

3 For there is forgiveness with you; *
   therefore you shall be feared.

4 I wait for you, O Lord; my soul waits for you; *
   in your word is my hope.

5 My soul waits for the Lord,
   more than sentries for the morning, *
   more than sentries for the morning.

6 O Israel, wait for the LORD, *
   for with the LORD there is mercy;

7 There is plenteous redemption with the LORD, *
   who shall redeem Israel from all their sins.

131

1 O LORD, I am not proud; *
   I have no haughty looks.

2 I do not occupy myself with great matters, *
   or with things that are too hard for me.

3 But I still my soul and make it quiet,
   like a child upon its mother's breast; *
   my soul is quieted within me.

4 O Israel, wait upon the LORD, *
   from this time forth for evermore.

132

1 LORD, remember David, *
   and all the hardships he endured;

2 How he swore an oath to the LORD *
   and vowed a vow to the Mighty One of Jacob:

3 "I will not come under the roof of my house, *
   nor climb up into my bed;

4 I will not allow my eyes to sleep, *
   nor let my eyelids slumber;

5 Until I find a place for the LORD, *
   a dwelling for the Mighty One of Jacob."

6 "The ark! We heard it was in Ephratah; *
   we found it in the fields of Jearim.

7 Let us go to God's dwelling place; *
   let us fall upon our knees before God's footstool."

8 Arise, O LORD, into your resting-place, *
   you and the ark of your strength.

9 Let your priests be clothed with righteousness; *
   let your faithful people sing with joy.

10 For your servant David's sake, *
   do not turn away the face of your anointed.

11 The LORD has sworn an oath to David, *
   and in truth will not break it:

12 "A son, the fruit of your body *
   will I set upon your throne.

13 If your children keep my covenant
   and my testimonies that I shall teach them, *
   their children will sit upon your throne for evermore."

14 For the LORD has chosen Zion *
   and desired it for the holy habitation:

15 "This shall be my resting-place for ever; *
   here will I dwell, for in Zion I delight.

16 I will surely bless the provisions of Zion, *
   and satisfy its poor with bread.

17 I will clothe its priests with salvation, *
   and its faithful people will rejoice and sing.

18 There will I make the horn of David flourish; *
   I have prepared a lamp for my anointed.

19 As for his enemies, I will clothe them with shame; *
   but as for him, his crown will shine."

133

1 Oh, how good and pleasant it is, *
   when the community lives together in unity!

2 It is like fine oil upon the head *
   that runs down upon the beard,

3 Upon the beard of Aaron, *
   and runs down upon the collar of his robe.

4 It is like the dew of Hermon *
   that falls upon the hills of Zion.

5 For there the LORD has ordained the blessing: *
   life for evermore.

134

1 Behold now, bless the LORD, all you servants of the LORD, *
   you that stand by night in the house of the LORD.

2 Lift up your hands in the holy place and bless the LORD; *
   the LORD who made heaven and earth bless you out of Zion.

135

1 Hallelujah!
  Praise the name of the LORD; *
   give praise, you servants of the LORD,

2 You who stand in the house of the LORD, *
   in the courts of the house of our God.

3 Praise the LORD, for the LORD is good; *
   sing praises to the name of God, for it is lovely.

4 For the LORD has chosen Jacob *
   and taken Israel as a possession.

5 For I know that the LORD is great, *
   and that our Lord is above all gods.

6 The LORD does whatever the LORD wills, in heaven and on earth, *
   in the seas and all the deeps.

7 The LORD brings up rain clouds from the ends of the earth, *
   sends out lightning with the rain,
   and brings the winds out of heaven's storehouse.

8 It was the LORD who struck down the firstborn of Egypt, *
   the firstborn both of humans and beasts.

9 The LORD sent signs and wonders into the midst of you, O Egypt, *
    against Pharaoh and all his servants.

10 The LORD overthrew many nations *
    and put mighty rulers to death:

11 Sihon, king of the Amorites,
    and Og, the king of Bashan, *
        and all the realms of Canaan.

12 The LORD gave their land to be an inheritance, *
    an inheritance for Israel, the chosen people.

13 O LORD, your name is everlasting; *
    your renown, O LORD, endures from age to age.

14 For you, O LORD, give your people justice *
    and show compassion to your servants.

15 The idols of the heathen are silver and gold, *
    the work of human hands.

16 They have mouths, but they cannot speak; *
    eyes have they, but they cannot see.

17 They have ears, but they cannot hear; *
    neither is there any breath in their mouth.

18 Those who make them are like them, *
    and so are all who put their trust in them.

19 Bless the LORD, O house of Israel; *
    O house of Aaron, bless the LORD.

20 Bless the LORD, O house of Levi; *
    you who fear the LORD, bless the LORD.

21 Blessed be the LORD out of Zion, *
    who dwells in Jerusalem.
        Hallelujah!

136

1 Give thanks to the LORD, who is good, *
    for the mercy of God endures for ever.

2 Give thanks to the God of gods, *
   for the mercy of God endures for ever.

3 Give thanks to the Lord of lords, *
   for the mercy of God endures for ever.

4 Who only does great wonders, *
   for the mercy of God endures for ever;

5 Who by wisdom made the heavens, *
   for the mercy of God endures for ever;

6 Who spread out the earth upon the waters, *
   for the mercy of God endures for ever;

7 Who created great lights, *
   for the mercy of God endures for ever;

8 The sun to rule the day, *
   for the mercy of God endures for ever;

9 The moon and the stars to govern the night, *
   for the mercy of God endures for ever;

10 Who struck down the firstborn of Egypt, *
   for the mercy of God endures for ever;

11 And brought out Israel from among them, *
   for the mercy of God endures for ever;

12 With a mighty hand and a stretched-out arm, *
   for the mercy of God endures for ever;

13 Who divided the Red Sea in two, *
   for the mercy of God endures for ever;

14 And made Israel to pass through the midst of it, *
   for the mercy of God endures for ever;

15 But swept Pharaoh and his army into the Red Sea, *
   for the mercy of God endures for ever;

16 Who led the chosen people through the wilderness, *
   for the mercy of God endures for ever;

17 Who struck down great rulers, *
	for the mercy of God endures for ever;

18 And slew mighty kings, *
	for the mercy of God endures for ever;

19 Sihon, king of the Amorites, *
	for the mercy of God endures for ever;

20 And Og, the king of Bashan, *
	for the mercy of God endures for ever;

21 And gave away their lands for an inheritance, *
	for the mercy of God endures for ever;

22 An inheritance for Israel, the chosen servant, *
	for the mercy of God endures for ever;

23 Who remembered us in our low estate, *
	for the mercy of God endures for ever;

24 And delivered us from our enemies, *
	for the mercy of God endures for ever;

25 Who gives food to all creatures, *
	for the mercy of God endures for ever.

26 Give thanks to the God of heaven, *
	for the mercy of God endures for ever.

137

1 By the waters of Babylon we sat down and wept, *
	when we remembered you, O Zion.

2 As for our harps, we hung them up *
	on the trees in the midst of that land.

3 For those who led us away captive asked us for a song,
	and our oppressors called for mirth: *
	"Sing us one of the songs of Zion."

4 How shall we sing the LORD's song *
	upon an alien soil?

5 If I forget you, O Jerusalem, *
   let my right hand forget its skill.

6 Let my tongue cleave to the roof of my mouth
  if I do not remember you, *
   if I do not set Jerusalem above my highest joy.

7 Remember the day of Jerusalem, O LORD,
  against the people of Edom, *
   who said, "Down with it! down with it!
   even to the ground!"

8 O city of Babylon, doomed to destruction, *
  happy the one who pays you back
  for what you have done to us!

9 Happy shall they be who take your little ones, *
  and dash them against the rock!

138

1 I will give thanks to you, O LORD, with my whole heart; *
  before the gods I will sing your praise.

2 I will bow down toward your holy temple
  and praise your name, *
   because of your love and faithfulness;

3 For you have glorified your name *
  and your word above all things.

4 When I called, you answered me; *
  you increased my strength within me.

5 All the rulers of the earth will praise you, O LORD, *
  when they have heard the words of your mouth.

6 They will sing of the ways of the LORD, *
  that great is the glory of the LORD.

7 The LORD is high, yet the LORD cares for the lowly *
  and perceives the haughty from afar.

8 Though I walk in the midst of trouble, you keep me safe; *
   you stretch forth your hand against the fury of my enemies;
   your right hand shall save me.

9 O LORD, you will make good your purpose for me; *
   O LORD, your love endures for ever;
   do not abandon the works of your hands.

139

1 LORD, you have searched me out and known me; *
   you know my sitting down and my rising up;
   you discern my thoughts from afar.

2 You trace my journeys and my resting-places *
   and are acquainted with all my ways.

3 Indeed, there is not a word on my lips, *
   but you, O LORD, know it altogether.

4 You press upon me behind and before *
   and lay your hand upon me.

5 Such knowledge is too wonderful for me; *
   it is so high that I cannot attain to it.

6 Where can I go then from your Spirit? *
   where can I flee from your presence?

7 If I climb up to heaven, you are there; *
   if I make the grave my bed, you are there also.

8 If I take the wings of the morning *
   and dwell in the uttermost parts of the sea,

9 Even there your hand will lead me *
   and your right hand hold me fast.

10 If I say, "Surely the darkness will cover me, *
   and the light around me turn to night,"

11 Darkness is not dark to you;
   the night is as bright as the day; *
   darkness and light to you are both alike.

12 For you yourself created my inmost parts; *
    you knit me together in my mother's womb.

13 I will thank you because I am marvelously made; *
    your works are wonderful, and I know it well.

14 My body was not hidden from you, *
    while I was being made in secret
    and woven in the depths of the earth.

15 Your eyes beheld my limbs, yet unfinished in the womb;
    all of them were written in your book; *
    they were fashioned day by day,
    when as yet there was none of them.

16 How deep I find your thoughts, O God! *
    how great is the sum of them!

17 If I were to count them, they would be more in number than
        the sand; *
    to count them all, my life span would need to be like yours.

18 Oh, that you would slay the wicked, O God! *
    You that thirst for blood, depart from me.

19 They speak despitefully against you; *
    your enemies take your name in vain.

20 Do I not hate those, O LORD, who hate you? *
    and do I not loathe those who rise up against you?

21 I hate them with a perfect hatred; *
    they have become my own enemies.

22 Search me out, O God, and know my heart; *
    try me and know my restless thoughts.

23 Look well whether there be any wickedness in me *
    and lead me in the way that is everlasting.

140

1 Deliver me, O LORD, from evildoers; *
    protect me from the violent,

2 Who devise evil in their hearts *
    and stir up strife all day long.

3 They have sharpened their tongues like a serpent; *
    adder's poison is under their lips.

4 Keep me, O LORD, from the hands of the wicked; *
    protect me from the violent,
    who are determined to trip me up.

5 The proud have hidden a snare for me
    and stretched out a net of cords; *
    they have set traps for me along the path.

6 I have said to the LORD, "You are my God; *
    listen, O LORD, to my supplication.

7 O Lord GOD, the strength of my salvation, *
    you have covered my head in the day of battle.

8 Do not grant the desires of the wicked, O LORD, *
    nor let their evil plans prosper.

9 Let not those who surround me lift up their heads; *
    let the evil of their lips overwhelm them.

10 Let hot burning coals fall upon them; *
    let them be cast into the mire, never to rise up again."

11 A slanderer shall not be established on the earth, *
    and evil shall hunt down the lawless.

12 I know that the LORD will maintain the cause of the poor *
    and render justice to the needy.

13 Surely, the righteous will give thanks to your name, *
    and the upright shall continue in your sight.

141

1 O LORD, I call to you; come to me quickly; *
    hear my voice when I cry to you.

2 Let my prayer be set forth in your sight as incense, *
    the lifting up of my hands as the evening sacrifice.

3 Set a watch before my mouth, O LORD,
  and guard the door of my lips; *
    let not my heart incline to any evil thing.

4 Let me not be occupied in wickedness with evildoers, *
    nor eat of their choice foods.

5 Let the righteous smite me in friendly rebuke;
  let not the oil of the unrighteous anoint my head; *
    for my prayer is continually against their wicked deeds.

6 Let their rulers be overthrown in stony places, *
    that they may know my words are true.

7 As when a plower turns over the earth in furrows, *
    let their bones be scattered at the mouth of the grave.

8 But my eyes are turned to you, Lord GOD; *
  in you I take refuge;
    do not strip me of my life.

9 Protect me from the snare which they have laid for me *
    and from the traps of the evildoers.

10 Let the wicked fall into their own nets, *
    while I myself escape.

142

1 I cry to the LORD with my voice; *
    to the LORD I make loud supplication.

2 I pour out my complaint before you, O LORD, *
    and tell you all my trouble.

3 When my spirit languishes within me, you know my path; *
    in the way wherein I walk they have hidden a trap for me.

4 I look to my right hand and find no one who knows me; *
    I have no place to flee to, and no one cares for me.

5 I cry out to you, O LORD; *
  I say, "You are my refuge,
    my portion in the land of the living."

6 Listen to my cry for help, for I have been brought very low; *
  save me from those who pursue me,
    for they are too strong for me.

7 Bring me out of prison, that I may give thanks to your name; *
  when you have dealt bountifully with me,
    the righteous will gather around me.

143

1 LORD, hear my prayer,
  and in your faithfulness heed my supplications; *
    answer me in your righteousness.

2 Enter not into judgment with your servant, *
    for in your sight shall no one living be justified.

3 For my enemy has sought my life,
  crushed me to the ground, *
    and made me live in dark places like those who are long dead.

4 My spirit faints within me; *
    my heart within me is desolate.

5 I remember the time past;
  I muse upon all your deeds; *
    I consider the works of your hands.

6 I spread out my hands to you; *
    my soul gasps to you like a thirsty land.

7 O LORD, make haste to answer me; my spirit fails me; *
    do not hide your face from me
    or I shall be like those who go down to the pit.

8 Let me hear of your loving-kindness in the morning,
  for I put my trust in you; *
    show me the road that I must walk,
    for I lift up my soul to you.

9 Deliver me from my enemies, O LORD, *
    for I flee to you for refuge.

10 Teach me to do what pleases you, for you are my God; *
    let your good Spirit lead me on level ground.

11 Revive me, O LORD, for you name's sake; *
    for your righteousness' sake, bring me out of trouble.

12 Of your goodness, destroy my enemies
    and bring all my foes to naught, *
    for truly I am your servant.

144

1 Blessed be the LORD my rock! *
    who trains my hands to fight and my fingers to battle;

2 My help and my fortress, my stronghold and my deliverer, *
    my shield in whom I trust,
    who subdues the peoples under me.

3 O LORD, what are we that you should care for us? *
    mere mortals that you should think of us?

4 We are like a puff of wind; *
    our days are like a passing shadow.

5 Bow your heavens, O LORD, and come down; *
    touch the mountains, and they shall smoke.

6 Hurl the lightning and scatter them; *
    shoot out your arrows and rout them.

7 Stretch out your hand from on high; *
    rescue me and deliver me from the great waters,
    from the hand of foreign peoples,

8 Whose mouths speak deceitfully *
    and whose right hand is raised in falsehood.

9 O God, I will sing to you a new song; *
    I will play to you on a ten-stringed lyre.

10 You give victory to rulers *
    and have rescued David your servant.

11 Rescue me from the hurtful sword *
and deliver me from the hand of foreign peoples,

12 Whose mouths speak deceitfully *
and whose right hand is raised in falsehood.

13 May our sons be like plants well nurtured from their youth, *
and our daughters like sculptured corners of a palace.

14 May our barns be filled to overflowing with all manner of crops; *
may the flocks in our pastures increase by thousands and
tens of thousands;
may our cattle be fat and sleek.

15 May there be no breaching of the walls, no going into exile, *
no wailing in the public squares.

16 Happy are the people of whom this is so! *
happy are the people whose God is the LORD!

145

1 I will exalt you, O God my Sovereign, *
and bless your name for ever and ever.

2 Every day will I bless you *
and praise your name for ever and ever.

3 Great is the LORD and greatly to be praised; *
there is no end to your greatness.

4 One generation shall praise your works to another *
and shall declare your power.

5 I will ponder the glorious splendor of your majesty *
and all your marvelous works.

6 They shall speak of the might of your wondrous acts, *
and I will tell of your greatness.

7 They shall publish the remembrance of your great goodness; *
they shall sing of your righteous deeds.

8 The LORD is gracious and full of compassion, *
slow to anger and of great kindness.

9 O LORD, you are loving to everyone, *
      and your compassion is over all your works.

10 All your works praise you, O LORD, *
      and your faithful servants bless you.

11 They make known the glory of your reign *
      and speak of your power;

12 That the peoples may know of your power *
      and the glorious splendor of your reign.

13 Your reign is an everlasting reign; *
      your dominion endures throughout all ages.

14 O LORD, you are faithful in all your words *
      and merciful in all your deeds.

15 The LORD upholds all those who fall *
      and lifts up those who are bowed down.

16 The eyes of all wait upon you, O LORD, *
      and you give them their food in due season.

17 You open wide your hand *
      and satisfy the needs of every living creature.

18 O LORD, you are righteous in all your ways *
      and loving in all your works.

19 O LORD, you are near to those who call upon you, *
      to all who call upon you faithfully.

20 You fulfill the desire of those who fear you; *
      you hear their cry and help them.

21 O LORD, you preserve all those who love you, *
      but you destroy all the wicked.

22 My mouth shall speak the praise of the LORD; *
      let all flesh bless your holy name for ever and ever.

146

1 Hallelujah!
Praise the LORD, O my soul! *
 I will praise the LORD as long as I live;
 I will sing praises to my God while I have my being.

2 Put not your trust in rulers, nor in any child of earth, *
 for there is no help in them.

3 When they breathe their last, they return to earth, *
 and in that day their thoughts perish.

4 Happy are they who have the God of Jacob for their help! *
 whose hope is in the LORD their God;

5 Who made heaven and earth, the seas, and all that is in them; *
 who keeps faith for ever;

6 Who gives justice to those who are oppressed, *
 and food to those who hunger.

7 The LORD sets the prisoners free;
 the LORD opens the eyes of the blind; *
 the LORD lifts up those who are bowed down;

8 The LORD loves the righteous
 and cares for the stranger; *
 the LORD sustains the orphan and widow,
 but frustrates the way of the wicked.

9 The LORD shall reign for ever, *
 your God, O Zion, throughout all generations.
 Hallelujah!

147

1 Hallelujah!
How good it is to sing praises to our God! *
 how pleasant it is to honor the LORD with praise!

2 The LORD rebuilds Jerusalem *
 and gathers the exiles of Israel.

3 The LORD heals the brokenhearted *
   and binds up their wounds.

4 The LORD counts the number of the stars *
   and calls them all by their names.

5 Great is our LORD and mighty in power, *
   whose wisdom is beyond limit.

6 The LORD lifts up the lowly, *
   but casts the wicked to the ground.

7 Sing to the LORD with thanksgiving; *
   make music to our God upon the harp.

8 God covers the heavens with clouds *
   and prepares rain for the earth;

9 God makes grass to grow upon the mountains *
   and green plants to serve humankind.

10 God provides food for flocks and herds *
    and for the young ravens when they cry.

11 The LORD is not impressed by the might of a horse *
    and has no pleasure in the strength of a man;

12 But the LORD has pleasure in the God-fearing, *
    in those who await God's gracious favor.

13 Worship the LORD, O Jerusalem; *
    praise your God, O Zion;

14 For God has strengthened the bars of your gates *
    and blessed your children within you.

15 God has established peace on your borders *
    and satisfies you with the finest wheat.

16 God's command is sent out to the earth, *
    and the word of the LORD runs very swiftly.

17 God gives snow like wool *
    and scatters hoarfrost like ashes.

18 God scatters hail like bread crumbs; *
     who can stand against the cold of the LORD?

19 God's word is sent forth and melts them; *
     God's stormwinds blow, and the waters flow.

20 God's word is declared to Jacob, *
     God's statutes and judgments to Israel.

21 The LORD has not done so to any other nation; *
     to them God's judgments have not been revealed.
     Hallelujah!

148

1 Hallelujah!
   Praise the LORD from the heavens; *
   praise the LORD in the heights.

2 Praise the LORD, all you holy angels; *
   praise the LORD, all heavenly host.

3 Praise the LORD, sun and moon; *
   praise the LORD, all you shining stars.

4 Praise the LORD, heaven of heavens, *
   and you waters above the heavens.

5 Let them praise the name of the LORD, *
   who commanded, and they were created.

6 The LORD made them stand fast for ever and ever *
   and gave them a law which shall not pass away.

7 Praise the LORD from the earth, *
   you sea-monsters and all deeps;

8 Fire and hail, snow and fog, *
   tempestuous wind, obeying God's will;

9 Mountains and all hills, *
   fruit trees and all cedars;

10 Wild beasts and all cattle, *
    creeping things and winged birds;

11 Kings of the earth and all peoples, *
  rulers and all judges of the world;

12 Young men and women, *
  old and young together.

13 Let them praise the name of the LORD, *
  for the name of the LORD only is exalted,
  and the splendor of the LORD is over earth and heaven.

14 The LORD has raised up strength for the chosen people
  and praise for all loyal servants, *
    the children of Israel, a people who are near to the LORD.
    Hallelujah!

149

1 Hallelujah!
  Sing to the LORD a new song; *
    sing praise to God in the congregation of the faithful.

2 Let Israel rejoice in their Maker; *
  let the children of Zion be joyful in their Sovereign.

3 Let them praise God's name in the dance; *
  let them sing praise to the LORD with timbrel and harp.

4 For the LORD takes pleasure in the chosen people *
  and adorns the poor with victory.

5 Let the faithful rejoice in triumph; *
  let them be joyful on their beds.

6 Let the praises of God be in their throat *
  and a two-edged sword in their hand;

7 To wreak vengeance on the nations *
  and punishment on the peoples;

8 To bind their rulers in chains *
  and their nobles with links of iron;

9 To inflict on them the judgment decreed; *
  this is glory for all God's faithful people.
  Hallelujah!

150

1 Hallelujah!
 Praise God in the holy temple; *
  give praise in the firmament of heaven.

2 Praise God who is mighty in deed; *
  give praise for God's excellent greatness.

3 Praise God with the blast of the ram's-horn; *
  give praise with lyre and harp.

4 Praise God with timbrel and dance; *
  give praise with strings and pipe.

5 Praise God with resounding cymbals; *
  give praise with loud-clanging cymbals.

6 Let everything that has breath *
  praise the LORD.
  Hallelujah!